FROM
VERSAILLES
TO VICHY
The Third French
Republic, 1919-1940

EUROPE SINCE 1500: *A Paperbound Series*

FROM VERSAILLES TO VICHY

The Third French Republic, 1919-1940

Nathanael Greene

WESLEYAN UNIVERSITY

THOMAS Y. CROWELL COMPANY

NEW YORK / ESTABLISHED 1834

To the memory of Doris Wilde Greene

Preface

This slender volume is intended to be an introduction to the history of the Third Republic from France's apparent victory in the First World War to her defeat in the Second. Being a history of a regime, it is avowedly a political history, emphasizing political forms and developments but not neglecting the social, economic, and diplomatic aspects of the years in question. It does not attempt to analyze cultural history, although prominent writers are discussed insofar as they figure among the main lines of the history of the Republic. As is the case with the other volumes in this series, *From Versailles to Vichy* attempts to present a narrative essay while offering a synthesis of recent historical interpretation, but responsibility for overall interpretation must necessarily be my own. I have drawn freely from many historical studies, especially of the 1930s, and I have indicated my sources either in footnotes or in the bibliography. Any work of synthesis is bound to have a slightly anemic character, and the reader is strongly encouraged to investigate these sources himself.

The main themes—the impact of the military disaster and collapse of the Republic in 1940 upon historical interpretation of the years from 1919 to 1940, the social and economic underpinnings of the Republic, the fruitless search for security, the social turbulence and political instability that masked the profound stability of the Republic, and the crises of the 1930s—are set out in the first chapter. Certain of these themes have been examined in depth by historians over the past decade, but synthetic and general re-evaluations of the history of France during the interwar years have been, virtually by default, the property of sometime historians and retired journalists. One recent work, as massive as it is bewildering, counts personalities, mistresses, and blunder as the motor forces of French history, virtually to the exclusion of anything else. Perhaps my modest effort will serve as a partial antidote to that brand of history, especially since this work is directed to students and others not well acquainted with modern French history. Although this is not a book for specialists, it may prove useful to them, and I would hope that my views stimulate discussion and argument.

I am indebted to Professor Alexander Sedgwick of the University of Virginia for his counsel and criticism, and to Professor Morton Briggs of Wesleyan University for his advice and assistance. Special appreciation is owed to Mr. Stanley Duane, formerly editor of this series, under whose guidance this book was begun and completed, and to Mrs. Dorothy Hay, who ably typed the manuscript.

N.G.

Middletown, Conn.

Contents

1 / Introduction

"A BAD CONSCIENCE"

"The generation to which I belong has a bad conscience," wrote the eminent historian turned resistance-fighter Marc Bloch, "from laziness, from cowardice, we let things take their course." Written in the shadow of the defeat of 1940, this indictment of a generation of Frenchmen has had remarkable longevity. The events of 1940 have cut deeply into the collective consciousness of Frenchmen, perhaps never to be erased. Even today, what a man is in the eyes of his contemporaries may be based partly on his actions before and after the catastrophe; certainly few middle-aged Frenchmen can escape its impact, whether it be in their certainty that the defeat of 1940 was the most significant event of the twentieth century, as General André Beaufre has written, or whether it be simply their conviction that 1940 marks a decisive watershed in the history of modern France. The German triumph was much more than the military defeat of France, however humiliating defeat may have been. The year 1940 also marked the hapless collapse of a republic whose institutions, deeply rooted in a way of life, had withstood the test of change and attacks from its enemies with greater success than any French regime since 1789. Born as a consequence of the military defeat of the Second Empire in 1870, the Third Republic died by its own hand at Vichy in July 1940, when the National Assembly, in the aftermath of Nazi victory, voted full powers to the elderly Marshal Pétain so that a new regime, consonant with

1

the "new Europe" of Adolf Hitler, might be created amid the ruins of "liberty, equality, and fraternity."

Once interred, the Third Republic, especially in its last years, was attacked by its foes and by many of its former friends as a regime of decadence, timidity, and squalor. What had been an ideal was now seen only as an excuse for stagnation, selfishness, and official hypocrisy. For the men of the Right, the Republic itself was the source of the shame of 1940; its institutions, they argued, had served only as a masterly cover for the politicians to deny the real France her right to life. On the Left, the failure of the Republic was alleged to have been the failure of the bourgeoisie, the reigning class, to fulfil the promises of Republicanism embodied in the motto "liberty, equality, and fraternity." In substance, the multiple indictment leveled against the Republic has become something of a black legend. Marc Bloch's bitter appraisal of his generation is characteristic not only of historical interpretation of the interwar years but also of the judgment of later generations who, somewhat ashamed of their fathers, find only in the social tumult of the late 1930s the saving grace of their forebears. The door has been shut on the interwar years, and the verdict apparently rendered, although intensive historical inquiry has been undertaken in the past decade. The interwar years were neither happy nor heroic, and they concluded in disaster.

Of what, then, does this multiple indictment consist? Intertwined, the indictments reveal a France of devastating parochialism, even to the point of prideful cultural self-sufficiency; a nation turned inward toward herself, obsessed with her international security yet weakened as all of her defenses were stripped away, including her self-reliance; a nation divided against itself, with a political system increasingly out of gear with reality. And they betray the grief of humiliation, embodied in the then-popular joke: "Why is it that France is ruled by seventy-five-year-olds? Because the eighty-year-olds are dead." It is instructive to open the dossier briefly here because its contents will be at the core of our own inquiry and effort to comprehend the troubled years from Versailles to Vichy.

The major criticism is familiar enough: France lacked the audacity and the willingness to act against the new barbarism represented by international fascism until it was too late, and then her liberation could not be her work alone. Symbolic of her comfortable security against European concerns was the famous Maginot Line, a massive defensive installation ranging along her German frontier. Constructed out of prudent fear of her powerful neighbor, the Line conveyed the image of fortress France, secure but apprehensive. Military plans, developed by the ossified minds that had fought the First World War and had drawn their lessons therefrom, were committed to defense, and defense alone. Hence France was deprived of the means to save her allies in central and eastern Europe, some of which were the obvious targets of the Nazi appetite. Furthermore, in 1940, once the German armies had skirted the Maginot fortifications by the simple device of crossing through Belgium, the lumbering French military machine was hopelessly outclassed by the lightening speed and easy mobility of the invader. Similarly, French diplomacy followed a downward course from blustery independence, as exemplified by the unilateral occupation of the Ruhr in 1923 in response to an alleged German refusal to fulfil the terms of the Treaty of Versailles, to outright and ignominious dependence upon another power, as demonstrated by her subordination to Great Britain in the Czechoslovakian crisis of 1938. From a power policy based on weakness to appeasement based on fear: such was the dismal record of France's statesmen.

Familiar too are the charges levied against France's political system and her politicians, the one designed to meet the needs of another epoch, and the other firmly committed to keeping the system mired in that epoch. Compromise and political maneuvering in the 1870s had determined that democracy in France was bound up with an all-powerful parliament, a Premier and his ministers highly vulnerable to the shifting sands of parliamentary politics, and a President whose official duties were largely confined to presiding at racetracks and flower exhibitions. Although some scholars who have peered deeply into the maze of political parties have concluded that there existed only two basic tendencies, one of movement, dedicated to political emancipation and modest social amelioration via state action, and one of order, devoted to holding tightly to the political and social status quo, the interwar years saw five or six political groupings, each roughly representative of a well-defined segment of society, competing for the allegiance of the electorate, and witnessed the emergence of several extraparliamentary groups whose aims were political but whose actions were not confined to the electoral arena. Thus the political formula seemed both unchanging and uninspiring: a multiplicity of parties, ministerial instability—one cabinet lasted only four days—and politicians doggedly determined to fight the battles of the past. Such a system and cast of characters were not prepared to withstand the crises of the 1930s.

It is alleged that fervent debate about, and apparent devotion to, shopworn ideologies deliberately masked social realities that betrayed the promises of Republicanism. France indeed was a compartmentalized society, where men lived and thought in separate groups, whether they were of class, profession, or trade. Bourgeois France admitted of distinctions, gradations, and even of hierarchy within itself, but most middle-class people rigidly separated themselves from the working class, which they characterized as a swamp from which very few ever escaped. Peasant France, itself divided into social layers according to the modes of agricultural exploitation, was united only by the rhetoric of ruralism, by the praise of rural life constantly sung by the politicians and certain "philosophers," and by the unfortunate conviction that independent work was the only work well done. Peasants and bourgeoisie were as one in an unspoken conspiracy of omission directed at the proletariat, whose hopes were minimal and whose exclusion from the national consensus was a *sine qua non* of this society. At the core of this consensus, it is argued, was an exaggerated individualism, an ethic so strong and so assiduously cultivated in almost every aspect of human activity that it paralyzed communication between individuals and between sectors of society, and prevented the development of necessary group endeavors. Hence, as Stanley Hoffmann has argued,[1] France was a "stalemated" society, static, lacking in dynamism, and, at least until after 1940, incapable of generating much-needed change. Society in France was not built around the business establishment, but around individualism on the one hand, and clusters of interests on the other.

A pioneer of the industrial revolution, France seemed to have become by the interwar years an economic backwater where bigness was considered an illness and small production units the model system. Comforting was the illusion of the permanence of smallness, as France remained a nation of petty producers and retailers despite the corroding effects of the World War, which had involved a certain rationalization and concentration of industrial activity. Happy were those who thought that emphasis on quality over quantity would insure immunity from the great depression that began in 1929, at least as long as smallness warded off the first waves of economic disaster. When the depression did hit, and when the illusion should have been shattered, France entered a period of economic hardship that endured longer than in other major Western nations, and for which France's economists, financiers, and politicians offered only the remedies of the past, and could not agree upon which of them to employ. Virtually throughout the interwar years France was plagued by the threat—and at least twice by the fact—of financial crisis, due partly to an inadequate tax structure, and paradoxically to the lack of confidence in France's economy by those who preached the virtues of smallness. Precipitating a financial crisis was also a major weapon in the political arsenal of the Right, and was used effectively to bring down governments of the Left.

These criticisms, and many more, comprise the basis of the dossier against the France of the interwar years. For some, France was simply a tired, lethargic nation, bled white by the First World War; she seemed incapable of producing men of quality. It was almost as if the second string were on the field for an

[1] Stanley Hoffmann, "Paradoxes of the French Political Community," in Stanley Hoffmann *et al., in Search of France* (Cambridge, Mass., 1963).

entire generation. Resistant to innovation and overly fond of the struggles of yesterday, France slipped deeper into a crisis whose final chapters, written in shame, were of a nation helplessly divided against itself in the 1930s and then overwhelmed in 1940. Yet some have suggested that the history of France in this era cannot be written apart from the same era in European history, a period of disaster for the old continent, when violence and action replaced rationality and progress as the dominant beliefs of all too many men. Hence the durability of French Republican forms and ideals in a Europe where dictatorship and totalitarianism seemed normal and inevitable may have been no small feat. As the great Socialist Léon Blum, himself a victim of the Republican system, has observed: "If all countries had had our wretched regime, differences would have been settled by negotiation." But decadence and decline persist as the prevailing themes of the years from France's apparent victory in the First World War to her defeat in the Second, years that are much more than the subject of historical curiosity for those who lived them and for those who may profit from learning about them.

"A HAPPY COUNTRY"

France's great political scientist André Siegfried once wrote that "France was a happy country." Presumably he was referring to an earlier segment of the history of the Third Republic, when politics seemed to pit the forces of enlightenment against a retrograde coalition of royalists and clerics, and when victory of the former seemed assured given time, resolution, and opportunity for a heady dose of Republican idealism to filter through all layers of society. Certainly by the dawn of the twentieth century the Republic had grown ample popular roots and appeared immune to assaults from the old Right, safely cast back into historical darkness after the Dreyfus affair, and whose partisans were now restricted to the pen in lieu of force. The Socialist and syndicalist Left, pugnacious in language and sometimes in action, was undermined by its own interminable divisions and paralyzed by conflicting aspirations. Even the Radicals, once regarded as extreme proponents of democratic liberalism, had been tamed by time and by participation in politics. Hence France was basically Republican, and some could say that indeed she was a happy country, relatively prosperous, a place where men who believed themselves to be free could place their confidence in progress.

Obviously Republican consensus excluded some, and others were self-excluded; but by the first years of this century a regime that had had at its birth the dubious distinction of being the form of government that least divided Frenchmen had settled into comfortable respectability. Since the Revolution, French politics had been marked by the interplay of at least four different political beliefs, which, for the sake of simplicity, we might label the counterrevolutionary, the conservative liberal, the democratic liberal, and the socialist. Surely there were many strands within each, and all mustered and lost support at different times across the nineteenth century; but each in itself, as a tradition, and as a basis of new political beliefs, had acquired permanent status.

Counterrevolution, associated with aristocratic *emigrés* who directed their wrath against revolutionary turmoil from across the Rhine during the Revolution, emerged as the dominant political trend after the defeat of Napoleon in 1815, had its heyday under the unfortunate reign of Charles X, who was toppled by the revolution of 1830, and resurfaced during periods of crisis, as in 1848 and 1871 to 1875. Counterrevolution means just what it says: an undying opposition to the central message of the Revolution, civil equality, combined with a conviction that the Revolution had diverted France from the course of history by upsetting the natural order of things—social hierarchy, a rural society based on the feudal myth of reciprocal rights and obligations of lord and servant, and a king who, while ruling as God's viceregent, is assisted in his tasks by a loyal but powerful aristocracy. Whatever the guise, from Charles X's attempt to recreate the past by alliance of throne and altar, via Charles Maurras' verbal assaults upon the Third Republic, to the fascists of the 1930s, the words inscribed on the counterrevolutionary banner remained the same: hierarchy, order, and authority.

Conservative liberals were more often than not the embarrassed heirs of revolution. Owing their legitimacy to the Revolution, they found it difficult to deny the legitimacy of revolution itself as a natural political procedure. Whether they were, like Guizot, men of the July Monarchy, so named after the July 1830 revolution, or like Thiers, who crushed the revolutionary Paris Commune in 1871, or the wary politicians of the Third Republic who feared social legislation as much as social upheaval, they were united in their will to end the revolutionary process. Descended from the Girondins of the Revolution, conservative liberals put their wager on a narrow political liberalism—equality before the law, representative institutions, sovereignty of the nation—and social conservatism. "Legal equality yes, social equality never!" might well summarize their liberal creed. Under the July Monarchy the essential problem had been how to insure political freedom without majority rule. Operating under a restrictive franchise, meaning that electors had to be men of substance, the July Monarchy bequeathed two fundamental things to the Third Republic. The first was the existence of a political class—the wealthy under the July Monarchy, the parliamentarians themselves under the Third Republic—who represented, indeed personified, the very essence of the nation. But what was the nation? It certainly was not the sum of all of its citizens, nor of all their wills; the nation was essentially an abstraction embodied in the parliament, and thus each parliamentarian spoke in theory not for his class, or his district, but for all. In fact the real country—the people—abdicated their power to the legal country—the parliamentarians—and sovereignty resided in parliament, which theoretically was omniscient. The second bequest mitigated the impact of the first: under the July Monarchy the king was not really necessary, serving only as a guardian against a parliament that might try to employ all of its theoretical power. Here was a real link to the Third Republic—the assumption that the state would not act, but would preserve and defend things as they were. Most conservative liberals and they should be labeled simply conservatives during the interwar years, were confident that a state limited to protecting the rights of its citizens was the latest model in perfection, if not the final product; and too often the conservative creed was translated to mean that homogeneous mediocrity was the stuff of good government and the orderly conduct of affairs.

Democratic liberals traced their inheritance to the Jacobins of the Revolution, especially to the Jacobin insistence upon the sovereignty of the people, which permitted them to concentrate on political matters, frequently to the exclusion of social concerns. From certain revolutionaries of 1848 via Léon Gambetta, the champion of Republicanism under Napoleon III, to the Radical chief Georges Clemenceau in the first half-century of the Third Republic, democratic liberals were fervent in their rhetoric but timid in their deeds; theirs was a revolutionary impulse tempered by a firm grip upon reality. Employing the symbols of the Revolution, democratic liberals were convinced that a republic based on universal suffrage, aided by time and by education of the people, would represent the apex of progress. One needed only to root out the vestiges of an unwholesome past and to strike down the enemies of enlightened liberalism in order for democracy—based on civil equality, equal political opportunity, and representative institutions in which each representative spoke for all of the nation—to prepare the way for unlimited happiness. Thus democratic liberals were at their most active when on the offensive against their enemies, especially against the Church, which they saw as an unremitting opponent of all liberal values. The Church, of course, replied in kind, and anti-clericalism served as a splendid rallying ground for all liberals, whatever their particular brand of liberalism. Especially necessary was the liquidation of Church dominance in education; the priests of Rome were to be supplanted by the lay teachers, the priests of the new religion of democracy. Thus, many of the struggles of the early years of the Republic had centered on control of education. Democratic liberalism had a definite touch of finality about it; once the Republic was a going concern, as it most certainly was by the first years of this century, democratic liberals were more concerned with protecting and preserving the present than with innovating, especially if innovation involved social change. Only the imperative of Republican defense would awaken the democratic liberals of the interwar years, the Herriots, Daladiers, and the Chautemps, to the need for social amelioration. Placing its faith in politics, democratic liberalism satisfied the needs and desires of most of the middle classes. Certainly it best embodied the popular idea that the Frenchman wore his heart on his left, and his pocketbook on his right.

The decade preceding the outbreak of the First World War was marked by a coalescence of conservative and democratic liberalism, and the product forged by this coalescence has been described by Stanley Hoffmann as the "Republican synthesis," which persisted as a viable political system until it collided with the crises of the 1930s. Beneath the surface turbulence of politics (which was distinguished by ideological fervor, especially over subjects that were not altogether relevant to the issues at hand, short-lived governments, and parliamentarians apparently zealous to share in the spoils of power), there ran a deep current of consensus, a current so strong that most political parties and parliamentary groups stood merely as sham rallying points for those who held fundamentally the same point of view. To regard the Republican synthesis as simply the compromise conclusion of the liberal family feud, or as a "Republic of pals," as the parliamentary game was derisively labeled by its critics, would be to underestimate the social basis of political attitudes. In fact the Republican synthesis was firmly rooted in social reality, and each served to reinforce the other, with the inevitable result of social and political stagnation.

What then were the structures and underlying beliefs of French society during the so-called golden years of the Third Republic, dating from about 1900 to sometime in the 1930s, and in what ways were they reflected in political beliefs, habits, and facts? The era has been stereotyped as *bourgeois* in economic matters and cultural trends as well as in politics, and indeed the middle classes placed their stamp upon those years. Defining *bourgeois* is less easy; it might best be described as a state of mind, a conviction of the majority of Frenchmen that they were more alike than different and that they shared certain values and occupied a certain status that differentiated them from the rest of their countrymen, especially from workers. It is not difficult to trace the emergence of the lesser bourgeoisie—small shopkeepers, white-collar workers, provincial lawyers and teachers, among others—as the political élite of the Third Republic. These were the people in whom Gambetta and democratic liberals had placed their hopes; but these people, once in power, simply desired a Republic that would protect and defend the interests of the "little men," themselves, and made no effort to espouse the cause of social equality or to sponsor state intervention to protect the weak. In this stalemated society, where mobility was accepted only within fixed limits, there existed a wide-ranging agreement among the middle classes on the necessity of preserving the social status quo. This fundamental agreement was expressed in a conception of life, in the cult of the family and of the individual, in the business structure, and in the structure of politics; and each of these prevailing beliefs and practices excluded the proletarian. This does not imply that France was a great industrial society, as were Great Britain, Germany, and the United States in the same era; the majority of the population before the First World War was rural and was engaged in agricultural pursuits, yet the nonproletarian population seems to have been obsessed with a fear of being proletarianized, and consequently erected barriers to stem the threat.

There was an enormous amount of inequality in French society, despite the motto of the regime and the Republican catechism propagated in the schools. A cult of bourgeois ideals or myths was taught officially and unofficially: the idea that the middle classes were in fact middle and average was accepted as self-evident; no one denied that a social hierarchy existed, but it was reasoned that upgrading within the hierarchy was always possible. Well-established traditions provided the cement of the middle classes: the family, it was thought, shaped the character of the child and shielded him from hostile outsiders, and because society was an individualistic war of all against all, the family was the only source of security. The family values of hard work and thrift, the backbone of the thousands of family enterprises, became an inviolable orthodoxy. In such a state of belief, bourgeois Frenchmen acted as a brake on the capitalist spirit: a premium on smallness, sanctification of the family business as the most respectable one, and the idea that thrift and refusal to take chances in the marketplace were marks of moral excellence meant not only the perpetuation of industrial adolescence but also of the bourgeois beliefs themselves.

Common values, aspirations, and fears were held by bourgeois and peasant alike. Winning the peasantry over to the Republic had been a major achievement of the Republicans, and the price of allegiance continued to be paid. In fact the coddling of the peasants by the politicians was simply the recognition of a historical fact. Formerly it had been assumed that Paris ruled France, and surely the Revolution itself had been primarily a Parisian affair; but since 1848, when provincial voters scuttled the hopes of Parisian revolutionaries, and since 1871, when almost all of France was at war with the revolutionary Paris Commune, the provinces had taken charge of their own destiny—and that of Paris. Politicians paid the political debt by praising agriculture as the basis of the French economy, peasant interests received friendly hearing in parliament, and peasant values were lauded as the values of civilization. It was precisely in their joint conception of work that peasant-bourgeois unity was maintained. The peasant, according to contemporary thinking, was the only real master of his labor, whereas the proletarian was not, and thus was deprived of his personality. If the bourgeois was not quite the master of his labor, he nonetheless was much closer to being so than the proletarian. What followed was a natural alliance of belief between bourgeois and peasant. Sharing the same values of hard work, thrift, and individuality, they were united in what they believed about life and in what they feared —the life of the proletarian. And they acted accordingly: if the peasantry, to borrow Stanley Hoffmann's terminology, served as a reservoir for entrance into the bourgeoisie, the proletariat remained stuck in a swamp, a situation the regime itself was well suited to maintain.

The "Republican synthesis," then, cannot be understood in

isolation from the "stalemated" society. The Republic, drawing upon the twin strands of liberalism, was to provide justice and to serve the common good, but it was not obligated to provide happiness or equality. Hence the paradox of a parliament theoretically sovereign—with the initiative lodged in the Chamber of Deputies, elected by universal manhood suffrage—checkmated by the widely shared understanding that the state would not go too far. In other words, the state's powers were carefully limited by the mentality of the stalemated society, by its overpowering desire to maintain the status quo. Although fear of a powerful leader can be traced to memories of the two Napoleons or to the conservative liberal concept of a weak executive, it seems more likely that French society did not want a strong leader or powerful group that might push the Republican synthesis and the stalemated society out of kilter. In any event, the Third Republic produced few great leaders, and then in time of crisis; they were honored only after they were safely dead.

No better example of the stability of the political system, as opposed to its surface instability, can be found than the Radical Party, the bearer of the democratic liberal tradition. It was at the hub of politics, from the close of the nineteenth century to the suicide of the Third Republic in 1940, with the exception of brief periods in the 1920s. The Radicals' actions betrayed the gulf between their leftist sentiments and their preference for stability and order; fervent in Republican rhetoric at election time, they were virtually indistinguishable from conservatives once in power. From Clemenceau to Daladier, Radicals slid toward the Right, as in 1934, when they dropped an uneasy partnership with Socialists to participate in a government led by a man of the Right, then slipped back again toward the Left, as in 1935. If this circuitous path was followed regularly, there were other constants of the Radical phenomenon. One was the very ambiguity of the party's organization, which was at best a loose combination of the local faithful grouped in committees, and at worst nonexistent. Another was an ingrained distrust of authority, best summarized by the unofficial philosopher of radicalism, Alain, who taught that the secret of government was "to obey but resist." The Radicals exhibited a permanent distrust of dynamic leadership and embraced a political philosophy that taught suspicion of politics and politicians. For the Radicals, and indeed for virtually all politicians, the major function of the deputy was to checkmate the ministers, to see that they did not damage the interests of their constituents. The function of the ministers was to oversee, not to lead, and to keep a watch on the bureaucracy, whose members, in their turn, regarded every client as a potential enemy and zealously guarded their own prerogatives by keeping watch on the ministers, sometimes undercutting them. The local committees served to keep the deputy in line, an admirable formula for inaction. The center of gravity of the Republican synthesis was not the government, but the deputy, and behind each deputy stood an alert committee. The whole system, in short, was geared to the absence of strong government; here was a system that would preserve the status quo and keep the Radicals' leftist inclinations from getting out of hand. Such a political system, resting upon firm social foundations, kept France locked in a pleasant but torpid stability.

Stability, obviously, was being purchased at a stiff price. If liberals were reconciled, and if Radicals and conservatives were able to march together under the umbrella of nationalism in the decade preceding 1914, there were disturbers of the domestic serenity, against whom the men of the Republican synthesis employed both promise and force, and not without success. The proletariat, ostracized from the majority of French society, had more than one movement and ideology vying to be its champion, although movements of and for the working class all drew inspiration from the Socialist strand of the Revolution. To simplify, in the ten years before 1914, two movements, socialism and syndicalism, drawing in differing degrees upon the promise of the Revolution—equality—and the revolutionary tradition of the French working class, sought to win over the workers. Socialism, represented after 1905 by the SFIO (*Section Française de l'Internationale Ouvrière*) sought to employ political means to realize its aspirations. Drawing upon several strands of the French and European socialist tradition—Marxist certainty of the inevitability of class warfare and the victory of the proletariat, the French revolutionary tradition, and working class self-sufficiency —plus the conviction that the French Revolution, which had brought about political emancipation, would be completed by and find its fulfillment in social emancipation, Socialists were committed to employing all means to launch the final revolution. Although internationalist by their own vows, Socialists in this decade were more a part of French political tradition than apart from it. Led by the great orator Jean Jaurès, the Socialist Party hoped to create social equality by progressive legislation and ultimately by a social revolution once it had captured political power, preferably by the ballot box. And for Jaurès, social revolution would not be to the exclusive benefit of the workers, but for the well-being of all Frenchmen. Hence the revolution would be the last chapter of the process begun in the Revolution of 1789. Peaceful and humanitarian in its deeds, and only occasionally violent in its rhetoric, the SFIO was essentially a party of democracy, asking only that its clients be admitted to the Republican family in fact as well as in theory.

Concentrating upon politics and political organization, by 1914 the SFIO had become the largest political party, recruiting workers, certain peasants and artisans, intellectuals, small-town teachers and lawyers, and some who voted habitually for the extreme Left. Despite its wide appeal, the Socialist Party, committed to patience rather than to action and to the political arena rather than the streets, was liable to the charge that it wanted only admission into the existing system and had scuttled revolution in its effort to do so. This charge was taken up by its competitor for working-class allegiance, the syndical and union organizations, headed by the CGT (*Confédération Générale du Travail*). Forsaking politics or collaboration with the Republic, syndicalist leaders sought to create a revolutionary consciousness among the workers by emphasizing the revolutionary tradition, itself bolstered by anarchist overtones, working-class self-help, and the belief that a massive general strike could be the most successful revolutionary weapon. In a country where union organization was difficult because of the intransigence of the owners and the great variety of small industrial units, the CGT was able to recruit only 4 per cent of the wage earners by 1906, but because unionism was weak the idea of revolution was attractive. As one syndicalist leader said, "Syndicalism does not waste time promising workers a paradise on earth: it calls upon them to conquer it." The years 1906 to 1909 were the "heroic period" of syndicalism, years in which the CGT helped foment strikes in the hope that the daily struggle would prepare the proletarian appetite for the final blow that would smash bourgeois society. The state, of course, replied with counterviolence, using force against strikes, so that after 1909 the CGT was compelled to dampen its revolutionary ardor in order to attempt to win economic gains for workers. Syndicalism as a doctrine and as an independent force seemed swallowed up by the First World War, but as a spirit, as an aspiration for total revolution by the workers themselves, it was to re-emerge with vigor in the immediate postwar years.

If socialism seemed tamed and syndicalism broken by 1914, the Republican synthesis was not free of enemies. On the extreme Right stood the modern guardians of the old values of hierarchy, order, and authority, declared enemies of the regime, armed with a modern ideology which some have seen as the first fascism. Unlike Adolf Hitler and Benito Mussolini, Charles Maurras did not have a great mass following, and he never captured state power; but he and his associates in the *Action Française* created a working, experimental model of a fascist movement, drawing upon the medley of hatreds, fears, and aspirations that was to be the reservoir of fascism after 1918. Maurras launched his lengthy journalistic and political career at the time of the Dreyfus affair at the close of the nineteenth century, when he entered the fray against Dreyfus, a Jewish army officer who had been wrongly accused and convicted of passing military secrets to the Germans. Finding Paris dominated by "Jews and foreigners," Maurras believed that the effort to exonerate Dreyfus was part of a plot by Jews and Republican politicians to crush the army, the last bastion of the values of eternal France. To fight the Republic, Maurras forged two very modern weapons: an ideology and a mass movement, although the former was more impressive than the latter. Relying heavily upon the counterrevolutionary tradition, Maurras rummaged through all of the political doctrines of the nineteenth century, and fabricated a doctrine designed to have a mass appeal. From the counterrevolutionaries Maurras borrowed the concept that a society must be managed by its elites —"democracy is evil, democracy is death"—but ruled by a single leader, the king, who incarnates the national destiny. From the Revolution Maurras simply took the view that revolution was a legitimate means to topple a decadent regime and that the masses must be included in the process of demolition.

Maurras called his ideology *integral nationalism,* and his arsenal of the moment wedded anti-Semitism to exaltation of violence and war. Like the Nazis, the *Action Française* had its street gangs, the *Camelots du Roi* crying "Death to the Jews"; Maurras believed that Jews were closely linked to the parliamentary republic and that Judaism itself was the carrier of all the diseases of modernity, from democracy to industrialism. The step from street gangs to powerful mass movement was too big for the *Action Française* to take, and the *Camelots du Roi* remained a safe haven for disgruntled middle-class youth, who engaged largely in symbolic actions, such as the desecration of Republican monuments and assaults on liberal professors. Although no immediate threat to the Republic, the *Action Française* stood by as the vocal representative of counterrevolution, and from its ranks emerged many of the fascist movements of the 1930s. By 1914 it offered revolution with safety, the opportunity to participate in an active movement sworn to destroy decadence while insuring one's own secure place in society; but it seemed incapable of mobilizing the final assault upon the Republic. Like the Socialists, the men of the *Action Française* were suspended in prerevolution.

France, then, may have been a "happy country." If happiness was not reserved for all, it was guaranteed for most by a stable regime resting upon a wide consensus, by middle-class beliefs, by the deception of liberal perfection, and at times by force. Backed by a great empire stretching from North Africa to Indo-

China and the Caribbean, alliance with Russia, and friendship with Great Britain, France appeared prepared to face her adversary across the Rhine should war erupt, although no one ever envisaged war on the scale of the 1914–1918 conflict. Cultural achievements had made Paris the capital of the intellectual world. The French economy, if quite inferior in productive capacity to those of other Western nations, certainly satisfied those who believed in its underlying premises. One could ask, however, as Robert Wohl has brilliantly done,[2] if the liberal system was living on borrowed time and by 1914 was perched on the edge of crisis. Certainly the Republican synthesis was a fragile construction, the product of the confluence of historical trends and conditions, suited only for the historical moment. Those who saw it as the climax of a long historical development and lived with the comforting illusion of its permanence failed to ask fundamental questions: How much could the Republican synthesis give in the way of social reform without ceasing to be a liberal system? To cite the reverse side of the coin, how long could the working class be marooned in its swamp without provoking a revolution? Finally, would social reform, let alone revolution, unleash a counterrevolution by the privileged that would destroy liberalism itself? The specter imposed by these questions does not take into account the impact of violence unchained that was the First World War. As we shall see in the following pages, the story of the interwar years was essentially that of the decline of the Republican synthesis. Badly scarred by war and revolution, and experiencing only a temporary convalescence in the 1920s, it cracked under the crises of the 1930s. And then all the long-postponed questions came to a head, at once making what had been a "happy country" a nation divided against itself, and faced with the terrible threat of Nazi Germany.

[2] Robert Wohl, *French Communism in the Making, 1914–1924* (Stanford, 1966).

2 / War and Peace

It took great ingenuity and vigilance in keeping French, Russians, and Germans interested in killing and being killed.

ROBERT WOHL

The First World War was the great unexpected crisis of this century, unexpected in that no one could have forecast the stupendous carnage, the unyielding stupidity of the sacrifice of millions of lives for mounds of worthless mud, the unprecedented destruction of cities, industries, and natural resources, and that rich fields would be made barren for eternity. Unexpected also was the still unfolding legacy of what was a European civil war: the abrupt disappearance of the old dynasties—Habsburg, Romanov, and Hohenzollern; the elevation of violence to respectability, almost as if violence was the preferable and normal mode of human behavior. Furthermore, 1914 was the beginning of an era of almost uninterrupted convulsion marked by two world wars and the threat of a third, a period of barbarism and inhumanity when the freedoms conquered in the nineteenth century were apparently freely surrendered. Finally, and perhaps most important, the several forces unleashed by the First World War mounted a powerful challenge against a whole system of belief and confident expectation.

In this sense 1917, not 1918, may have been the pivot of four years of holocaust. Nineteen-eighteen witnessed the conclusion of a bloodletting from which no European nation emerged victorious, despite shabby efforts by certain statesmen

19

to portray the war as an Allied triumph and the unrealistic effort of President Wilson to declare it a victory for democracy. Nineteen-seventeen introduced revolution into Russia, and the threat —or promise—of revolution across the continent. Powerless to prevent and then to halt the slaughter of the best of a generation, liberalism as a system and as a body of belief was called into question. Like the old monarchies, liberalism also seemed, for a brief moment, destined to be swept away. And France, the mother of revolution, was not to escape the new revolutionary tide, this time coming from the east.

LA GRANDE ILLUSION

Throughout the years 1914–1919 the majority of Frenchmen, including responsible public officials and presumably responsible military leaders, lived on a series of illusions about the great struggle upon which they had embarked. The first was that war was welcome and victory would be swift. In the summer of 1914 crowds swarmed through the streets of Paris crying "To Berlin!" and their enthusiasm was matched by an outpouring of patriotic and nationalist propaganda by the politicians. Even the Socialists temporarily abandoned pacifism and internationalism and signified their approval of a "just war" against alleged German aggression by participating in a *union sacrée* (sacred union) of all political parties in defense of the nation. The second illusion, a substitute for the first, which had worn thin by 1915, held by the military and some civilians alike, was that offensives, costing a fantastic total in lives and gaining precious little in territory, could be mounted continually until the enemy's lines were breached and this without provoking rebellion among the troops and political discontent at home. The third illusion, enjoyed after the cessation of hostilities in late 1918, was that the Germans would pay the cost of what had been a collective European folly, and that chauvinism and superpatriotism would be agreeable substitutes for social reform, thus permitting the reestablishment of the prewar domestic status quo.

There is no need to trace the military developments, from the "miracle of the Marne" in 1914, when the French lines held and prevented a German breakthrough to Paris, to the stalemate of 1915–1917, distinguished by the unspeakable loss of life at Verdun in 1916 and in the so-called Nivelle offensive in 1917, to the Armistice of November 11, 1918. Those developments are clear enough; the front in eastern France became a vast cemetery, a monument to man's stupidity rather than to his valor. France's losses in this reckless waste of lives are seen in this appalling tally: 1,400,000 men were killed at the front or of wounds suffered; 2,800,000 were wounded, of whom some 740,000 were maimed for life. If cold figures cannot convey the dimensions of the human tragedy of these four years, one need only visit the fortress of Verdun, where a huge ossuary has been constructed to hold the remains of the nearly 700,000 men of both sides who fell there; one should also gaze about the fields of Verdun, still unsafe to enter because of the presence of thousands of unexploded shells. Europe lost ten million lives in this war; France, with a population of forty million, suffered a more severe loss of her young than any other nation. Materially France also suffered: 800,000 dwellings demolished or damaged, 54, kilometers of roads destroyed, untold damage to her railways, industries, and mines by warfare and by the systematic vandalism of the retreating Germans in 1918.

French democracy also suffered during the war—at the hands of the conservative President of the Republic, Raymond Poincaré, who employed the slender powers of his office to preserve the fiction of unshakeable national union and to pursue the war at all cost, without dissension; at the hands of the old Radical wheelhorse, Georges Clemenceau, who as Premier subordinated everything, including individual liberty, to "making war"; at the hands of parliamentarians eager to push responsibilities on to others, even at the risk of abdicating some of their legitimate power; and at the hands of generals such as Joffre, who were impatient with the niceties of the democratic process. All were slow to recognize the deepening folly to which France had committed herself, and many saw the folly as a crusade; and all were equally slow to envisage ways to extricate France from the morass, and employed repression against those, like the politician Caillaux, who did.

At the outset of the war, from August through December 1914, the government and the military saw to it that fundamental liberties were exercised only by their permission. Under the *union sacrée* individual freedoms were curbed; the police powers of the state were increased; military court-martials for civilians, in which only twenty-four hours were allotted to prepare one's defense, became regular procedure; censorship was imposed and carried to new heights of rigor and foolishness under Clemenceau from late 1917 through the peace conference of 1919; and private enterprise was regulated and disciplined, although in a haphazard and often erratic manner. In short, the constitutional regime was voluntarily suspended in 1914. But from 1915 to Clemenceau's arrival to power, parliament slowly reasserted its authority, even to the point of investigating military actions, much to the annoyance of the military chiefs, and the removal of General Joffre from the High Command in 1916 represented the high-water mark of parliamentary power.

In 1917, the failure of General Nivelle—to whom parliament was quite sympathetic—to crack the German lines, plus the unedifying spectacle of government by elderly politicians and the fact of Bolshevik revolution in Russia, made it imperative to Poincaré that a man come to office who could galvanize the war effort, inspire public confidence, squash growing domestic dissent over the war, and end the demoralizing squabble between politicians and the military. Poincaré selected Clemenceau for this task, and the new Premier left no doubt as to his intention to rule with an iron fist. Clemenceau meant what he said when he declared "I make war." He waged war on his critics as well as on the Germans, and his government marked a decisive return to the executive firmness that had characterized the early days of the war. Supported by a public opinion that had been dismayed by parliamentary antics, Clemenceau was given authority in February 1918 to legislate by decree in economic matters. In the last year of the war the Clemenceau government had more authority than any in the history of the Third Republic, and this power was utilized not only to direct the war with vigor, revive public confidence, and enlarge the competence of the government in economic matters, but also to stifle criticism, especially from the growing number of Socialists who had sought, beginning with modest suggestions in 1915, to put a halt to the carnage. Thus parliamentarianism and democracy did not emerge unscathed from the war; the price to be paid was a popular wave of antiparliamentary and even antidemocratic sentiment.

REVOLUTION IN RUSSIA—AND IN FRANCE?

"It was the unchained nationalism unleashed by the bourgeoisie," writes Annie Kriegel, "that drove the working class toward Bolshevism." [1] By 1917, unchained nationalism offered the promise of unending carnage on the battlefields and repression of dissent at home; some French soldiers did mutiny, their only way to protest the obstinacy of their superiors, and certain politicians who dared suggest a compromise peace were hunted down, especially by Clemenceau. However, much more than reaction to unchained nationalism was involved in the French potential for Bolshevism and revolution. Weariness with the war and its horror was undoubtedly a major ingredient, as was the progressive splitting of the SFIO into pro- and antiwar camps, with the latter gaining ascendancy, although it was basically a pacifist and not a revolutionary group. The war also wrought economic and social changes that contributed heavily toward creating a new political situation. Also, by 1917–1918 there were many who were prepared to question all of the values of prewar society, and questioning led to challenge of those values. Against this background, it was all but inevitable that the Bolshevik Revolution of November 1917 would have repercussions in France. Riding a short but powerful wave of accumulated discontents in Russia, chief among which was an overwhelming desire to be done with a senseless war, Lenin came to power

[1] Annie Kriegel, *Aux Origines du Communisme français, 1914–1920* (Paris, 1964).

and proclaimed that his revolution was but the first installment of world revolution. From 1917 through 1919 the Bolshevik Revolution was to rival war and peace for the attention of Frenchmen, and by 1919, according to Robert Wohl, revolution was a mood that pervaded all levels of society.

Socialists, as we have seen, had placed their Socialist faith in the unfolding of the Republican promise, however illusory that choice may have been as long as social revolution remained their proclaimed goal. Deprived of their great leader Jaurès, who fell to an assassin's bullet on the very eve of war in 1914, Socialists rallied to the *patrie* in war, and some joined the government as representatives of their party. Years of antimilitarist and pacifist propaganda were swept away in a single moment. By 1915 disenchantment with the war, with the government's apparent determination to close its ears to possibilities of compromise peace, and with the conduct of certain Socialist leaders, equally deaf to hints of peace, led a minority of the SFIO to begin asking embarrassing questions about what was becoming endless warfare. These murmurs of discontent grew in 1916 and 1917 into an organized opposition to the war, although it was itself split over what tactics to pursue; one group moved into total opposition to the war, while a second urged discussions with Socialist parties of enemy countries as a first step toward terminating the war. By 1917, even the majority of Socialists who had supported the war fully in 1914 had moved back toward internationalism and in support of finding ways to a compromise peace, and when Socialists were denied passports by the government to attend an international conclave of Socialist parties, even the fiction of *union sacrée* was erased. Socialists were surprised by the Bolshevik Revolution, and most kept their opinions in abeyance; a minority was clearly stimulated by the Bolshevik victory, but the majority of Socialists feared that support of Bolshevik Russia's unilateral withdrawal from the war could expose them to the charge of antipatriotism. With Allied intervention in behalf of the Russian counterrevolutionaries in the summer of 1918, support of Lenin's revolution helped the antiwar minority displace the prowar majority leadership of the SFIO. By the time of the Armistice, then, the SFIO seemed to have broken its 1914 partnership with the bourgeois political parties, and the promise of revolution appeared to be on the horizon. Would pacifist and antiwar sentiment be translated into revolutionary sentiment?

Even if Socialists were suddenly to recover their will for revolution, it was not at all clear that conditions in France approximated, let alone duplicated those that had made for Bolshevik success in Russia. Lenin and his well-organized Bolsheviks had seized power in November 1917 from a weak and virtually nonexistent Provisional Government by playing upon popular hostility to the war, proletarian outrage and capacity for insurrection, and peasant discontent. Russia also had had no experience in liberal democracy, and a coherent revolutionary elite could easily supplant a discredited form of absolutism with its own absolutism. The victory of revolution in Russia, as well as the potential for similar revolution elsewhere in Europe at the close of the First World War, as in Germany, Hungary, and Italy, demonstrated that Bolshevism, when identified as a total challenge to existing authority and the beliefs underlying authority, was a European phenomenon. Four years of war, of violence, of inhumanity, and of destruction had simply put everything into question. But if the potential for revolution was widespread, it was clearly no guarantee that the Bolshevik feat would be repeated anywhere, least of all in France.

Certain conditions in France did in fact favor the development of a revolutionary situation. By 1918, Socialists had broken with the government over the war issue, and they were pushed along in 1919 by the growing radicalization of their followers, chiefly among the proletariat. The French proletariat, which had been shunted aside by the Republican synthesis and which since 1848 had been the active bearer of the revolutionary tradition, had become larger and more concentrated in large population centers during the war because of the demands imposed on industry by the war effort. By 1919 it had become a swollen, angry mass, susceptible to manipulation by a revolutionary elite. Syndicalist stirrings as early as 1916 had signalled the revival of working-class anger, and the Russian example appeared to prove that revolution was a viable alternative to social inequality masked by democracy and the murderous war that democracy did not know how to avoid or to stop. Early in 1919, with both SFIO and CGT deluged with impatient new followers, it seemed clear that persistent social turmoil could grow into revolution; as André Siegfried observed, the threat of Bolshevism absolutely terrified those who had something to lose. The government refused to pay the price of hefty social legislation to take the heart out of any revolutionary appeal, and instead resorted to the truncheon; Léon Jouhaux, the leader of the CGT, was himself assaulted by the police in May Day demonstrations. Continuing French intervention in Russia against the Bolsheviks made Bolshevism all the more attractive to many workers; "the workers," it has been said, "loved the Bolsheviks for their enemies." Thus the legacy of war and of history, embodied in strikes in which workers' banners praised the Bolshevik Revolution, coupled with government intransigence against far-reaching social legislation and its insistence upon fighting Bolsheviks in Russia, seemed to set the scene for an explosion, perhaps even a revolution.

Of course, revolution did not occur; if the raw materials were present to a degree, there was no one able to combine them into an assault upon existing society. Unlike Russia in 1917, France was not still bogged down in war in 1919, and she counted herself among the victors. The major task of a victorious government was to present the bill to the losers, and in so doing to lower the revolutionary fever by manufacturing and encouraging popular sentiments for revenge against and reparations from the defeated enemy. Unlike the spineless men of the Russian Provisional Government, France's rulers—Clemenceau, Poincaré, and after the election of 1919, Alexandre Millerand—were prepared to employ all the force of the state to crush revolution in the bud. Just the threat to call in troops in July 1919 forced the CGT to call off its plans for a general strike. Unlike in Russia, the forces of order—the police and the army—remained loyal to the regime. The politicians were not yet persuaded of their incapacity to rule, and perceived the challenge: the parties of the Center and the Right united under the threat of the "Red Menace," and won a handy victory in the election of 1919. By playing the card of fear, conservatives forged a coalition of the middle classes and emerged stronger in the Chamber than at any time since the early years of the Third Republic. The revolutionary effervescence of 1919 carried over to 1920, but it could not sustain its momentum. As Victor Griffuelhes, a syndicalist leader of the pre-war years, had observed: "The French working class has all the defects which characterize the Latin: the lack of follow-through and tenacity in action, which is made up of passing waves of wrath, which a little nothing arouses and a little nothing appeases. It has little endurance, not that it is incapable of endurance, but because it attaches more importance to the effort of an hour or of a day. For that effort it gives itself completely. Then if the effort is successful and brings results, everyone notes it, not dreaming that to maintain it action is necessary."

The failure of the strike of May 1920, as a result of which 22,000 workers lost their jobs, sealed the fate of revolution; fearful of losing what they did have, most workers passed back into passivity, not to be aroused again until 1936. Again unlike Russia, France did have a liberal democratic tradition, and the Republic, as an institution and as a promise, was not an untested provisional government. Finally, this Republic did have friends among the Socialists themselves. It was one thing to move into opposition to the war, but quite another to cut loose all moorings to the Republic. The Socialists simply did not produce a Leninist type of revolutionary elite until after the revolutionary wave had receded, and then only at the cost of bitter internal wrangling and division of the Socialist ranks. Many Socialists remained wedded to the ideals and expectations of Jaurès, never realizing that the failures of Jaurès' socialism had contributed much to the workers' admiration of Bolshevism in 1919; the gap between what the Jaurès' formula promised and what it had achieved was wide, and debate over its validity separated Socialists from Communists throughout the interwar years, or at least until 1934.

So the revolution was an abortive one, and this was perhaps inevitable; but the fear that it inspired was not to be forgotten quickly.

VERSAILLES

Peacemaking in 1919 has been one of the subjects most written about in modern history, and certainly the Treaty of Versailles, which fixed blame for the war squarely on Germany and established that she should pay reparations to the victors, is a subject of enduring controversy and continuing historical inquiry. Fifty years of debate have centered around the alleged failure of President Wilson to persuade the victors to share his idealism, and, also upon what has been described as morally unfair and economically disastrous treatment of Germany. Critics of the President have condemned his departures from principle in accepting a treaty that violated national self-determination and betrayed his implied promise of leniency to Germany if she were to cast off her monarchy and embrace democracy, which she did. Some have condemned Wilson outright for attempting to impose American middle-class views upon a Europe that may have been marching toward social emancipation. Defenders of Wilson argue that, given the hostilities and violence bred by war and the imperative demands of France, plus the impossibility of not hurting some nationalities at the expense of others, no better treaty could have been obtained; and, they add, the Treaty was all the better for Wilson's participation, especially in its inclusion of a League of Nations.

The treatment of Germany has been even more controversial. Those who believe it was too harsh point out that Germany was no more guilty than others in 1914. They argue that the Treaty was the root cause of the Second World War because it was imposed upon Germany and not negotiated with her; prescribed that reparations would be paid, even at the cost of her economic ruin; separated her eastern territories by a Polish corridor, inevitably a source of dispute; incorporated Germans into non-German states such as Czechoslovakia; and because it imposed severe limitations upon her military rights, such as the limitation of her army to 100,000 men. To the proponents of this view it is France, by the brutality of her demands and her unstinting obsession with security from Germany, that should shoulder the burden of blame for the Treaty. In response, others have pointed out that the Treaty was in fact too lenient, that it was unable to contain German propensity for aggression, and that it gave France no security at all; 1870, 1914, and 1940 are simply stages in German aggression against France. A. J. P. Taylor has pointed out that fulfillment of the Treaty,[2] including reparations, depended upon German willingness to comply, and that German statesmen, from those of the Weimar Republic through Hitler, progressively undid the provisions of the Treaty. Another school argues rather persuasively that the Treaty was the worst of all possible worlds: if Germany was to be held in check, then the Treaty should have been much stiffer and its fulfillment guaranteed by the victors; if Germany was to be integrated into a European family, then the Treaty should have been more lenient and not a persistent source of humiliation to Germans. Without entering deeply into the debate, we should examine the reasons for the French attitude and inquire whether she did receive either satisfaction or security from the Treaty.

France certainly had a good case against the Germans, and her chief negotiator at the peace conference, the tough Georges Clemenceau, was determined that the debt owed France be paid in full. His logic was as intransigent as it was apparently irrefutable: Germany had caused the war; the war in the West had been fought largely on French soil; damage done to France by war and German vandalism had to be repaired at German cost; having escaped heavy damage to her own territory, Germany could afford to make retribution; and because Germany stood indicted by her own past, her reliability as a trusted partner for peace was at best uncertain, requiring international safeguards against her capacity for military adventure. The provinces of Alsace and Lorraine, torn from France by German ag-

---

[2] A. J. P. Taylor, *The Origins of the Second World War* (London, 1961).

gression in 1870, should naturally be returned to their rightful owner. France had lost more of her young men proportionate to her population than had Germany, and it was evident that she would remain demographically inferior to Germany in the future. Germany clearly would retain her industrial supremacy over France. Clemenceau also could not escape the popular conviction that France's tremendous human losses demanded that Germany be deprived of the means to launch another war; the popular slogans "Never Again!" and "Our dead shall not have died in vain!" found their echo in Clemenceau's diplomacy. Yet such slogans were also an integral part of Clemenceau's politics. As Arno Mayer has shown,[3] the diplomacy of peacemaking in 1919 cannot be dissociated from the domestic politics of the Allied powers, and for most of France's politicians demands for a Draconian peace and preservation of the political and social status quo went hand in hand. With the social turbulence of 1919, the encouragement of popular clamor for justice and protection from Germany was an admirable foil against the possibility of revolution and it offered a shield behind which France could continue to aid the enemies of Bolshevism in Russia. Instead of social reforms, Germany would pay! Encouragement of nationalist and chauvinist sentiment is a time-honored method of channeling popular anger away from domestic issues, and this time was no exception. Finally, Clemenceau shared and drew upon another popular feeling: France had fought for victory, not to make the world safe for democracy—and she had won, or so Frenchmen believed.

There was considerable discrepancy between what Clemenceau demanded and what France received, a fact that was not overlooked when Clemenceau was denied the Presidency of the Republic in 1920. France insisted upon the return of Alsace-Lorraine; Germany's payment of the costs of the war by reparations—not by an indemnity, as the Germans had themselves prepared to require of the Allies had they won the war; the

[3] Arno Mayer, *Politics and Diplomacy of Peacemaking: Containment and Counterrevolution at Versailles, 1918–1919* (New York, 1967).

annexation of the Saar Basin to France; and, upon the insistence of the French military, the separation of the left bank of the Rhine from Germany. Most of the French demands were opposed or softened by Wilson and the British Prime Minister, David Lloyd George, the latter suffering not from an excess of idealism but from a growing concern that France's demands masked her desire to keep Germany perpetually weaker than France. Alsace-Lorraine's reattachment to France presented no problem, but Wilson balked in the case of the Saar, and the area was placed under international administration for fifteen years, with France given the right to exploit its coal mines. Wilson rejected the proposal that Germany pay the costs of the war, but agreed that Germany should be responsible for all civilian damages, the amount to be determined by 1921. Both Wilson and Lloyd George rejected separation of the left bank of the Rhine, and substituted Allied occupation of that area for fifteen years, provided for a thirty-mile-wide demilitarized strip on the right bank, and gave a joint British-American guarantee to France providing for their support in event of a German attack. As mentioned, the German army was limited to 100,000 men.

What security, then, had France achieved? Really nothing but the German signature to the Treaty. When Germany pleaded inability to pay reparations, France found that she could not force the Germans to pay. Germany easily evaded the limitations on the size of her army, and when Hitler boasted of the increase in the army, France had no recourse. When Hitler militarily reoccupied the Rhineland, France believed herself to be helpless to act; and the British-American guarantee was a dead letter from the moment the United States Senate failed to ratify the Treaty, thus releasing Britain from her obligation. Clemenceau was accused of having bartered substance—French forces permanently on the Rhine—for shadow—a guarantee quickly renounced by the guarantors. France's search for the security that she thought she deserved in 1919 extended throughout the interwar years; the search proved to be fruitless. Yet given the total diplomatic situation it would have been remarkable had Clemenceau won agreement to his original demands.

3 / The Politics
and Diplomacy
of Order,
1919-1929

Briand knows nothing and understands everything; Poincaré knows everything and understands nothing.

POPULAR OBSERVATION

The period of the 1920s in France generally has escaped the retrospective condemnation of the 1930s as a dismal if not desperate decade. Not that the 1920s were exciting or even memorable; the virtues of its great public figures, Raymond Poincaré and Aristide Briand, were as humdrum as their vices. Against the background of economic buoyancy, to be discussed in Chapter Four, the spirit and the systems of the past were successfully refloated; the quest for "normalcy" extended far beyond the shores of the conservative America of Harding, Coolidge, and Hoover. In its fundamental themes as in its political personnel, the 1920s were closer to the decade preceding the First World War than the decade that was to follow. It was a time of domestic tranquility managed by the men of order, interrupted only by an interlude of confused leftist rule, and disturbed by a passing financial crisis and the perplexing irritant of the search for international security. Issues thought settled were conveniently exhumed and flailed again, much to the satisfaction of the politicians who preferred to live in history than in the present. The Republican synthesis, once resurrected, again represented the politics of safety; renewed debate over the place of the Roman Catholic Church in French society was both a tonic and a stimulant to the political class, and it provided insurance against having to deal with real issues, such as economic modernization and social reform. As for the rebellious workers of 1919–1920, they returned to resigned patience, and their organizations engaged in fratricidal combat against each other. Domestic politics could not be divorced from foreign policy, and more than once both were closely intertwined, acting reciprocally upon the other. The search for order extended into foreign affairs, by force and by conciliation, and was without definitive result. This was a decade, then, of revival, distinguished by an uneasy retreat into the past, and of respite before the storms of the 1930s.

CONSERVATISM REVISITED: THE *BLOC NATIONAL*

Profiting from a medley of circumstances and their own keen sense of political realities, the men of the Center and Right won an overwhelming victory in the legislative election of 1919; not since 1876 had the center of gravity in the Chamber of Deputies been anchored so far toward the Right. Essentially the *Bloc National*, composed of the parties of the Right and Center, plus some Radicals, owed its triumph to chauvinism and fear of revolution, and it lived for more than four years on the hangover of *union sacrée* and the threat of Bolshevism. A new electoral system,[1] in which deputies were elected on a single ballot on a

[1] The old electoral system, restored for the elections of 1928, 1932, and 1936, was based upon single-member constituencies and two ballots, separated by a week—the second ballot being necessary if no candidate achieved an absolute majority on the first ballot; on the second ballot a plurality sufficed for election. This generally worked to the advantage of the leftist parties by permitting political trading and withdrawal of candidates during the week intervening between ballots, thereby permitting the

department-wide basis (departments are administrative units, about the size of a large American county), put a premium on organization and worked in favor of the *Bloc National,* which was much better organized than its opponents. The Radicals, for example, refused to ally with the Socialists, who seemed to them to be a bewildered party of second-hand revolution. Exploiting the popular conviction that "Germany must pay," the electoral tactics of the *Bloc National* effectively smothered serious debate; anti-Germanism welded together a popular electoral coalition convinced that reparations would ensure French recovery and social appeasement. A mild antiparliamentarianism was another ingredient in the successful prescription of the *Bloc.* Although some deputies had managed to get themselves killed during the war, the erosion of parliamentary authority in 1914–1918 and the authoritarian rule of Clemenceau made an appeal for men of action, strength, and order all the more plausible. Not that new faces were much in evidence—Poincaré himself was Premier from 1922 to 1924—and Alexandre Millerand and Aristide Briand were veteran politicians. Both Millerand and Briand, like Pierre Laval, the notorious collaborator with the Germans in 1940–1944, had travelled a curious path from socialism to the Center and Right, where political power rested, although Briand's flexibility still gave him credit on the Left, and he lived his reputed maxim "life is made of rubber" to the full. During its hold on power, from 1919 to 1924, the *Bloc National* was noteworthy for inaction at home and overreaction in foreign affairs.

The politics of inaction scored an initial triumph in the eviction of Clemenceau from the political arena. Clemenceau was a man of war, not peace, and was a potential disrupter of domestic tranquility. Hence he was denied election to the Presidency of the Republic by the National Assembly (the Senate and the Chamber of Deputies convened jointly), and he departed for a lonely and embittered retirement. Undoubtedly his

---

Left to present a single candidate against those of the Center and Right. In many constituencies, of course, this system worked to the advantage of the Center and Right, provided they could agree upon a single candidate for the second ballot.

defeat was due to several factors, chief among them dissatisfaction with his role in negotiating the Treaty of Versailles, but Clemenceau's fate was typical of the Third Republic: strong personalities were called only in time of crisis, and neither needed nor wanted otherwise. The election of his opponent, Paul Deschanel, proved to be an embarrassing error, as the new Chief of State soon displayed unmistakable signs of mental instability, and when he disappeared from a Paris to Marseilles train and subsequently was discovered in rather bizarre circumstances, he was compelled to resign. Alexandre Millerand was elevated to the Presidency, and persuaded that his post entailed duties richer than presiding at chrysanthemum exhibitions, he intervened actively in politics, ranging from undermining his Premier in 1922 to open participation in the electoral campaign in 1924.

In domestic affairs, the *Bloc National* did what conservative governments usually did and still do: it avoided innovation, kept taxes as low as the situation would tolerate, and maintained the fiction of a balanced budget. The income tax, adopted hastily and at a low rate during the war, was not increased to help pay the costs of reconstruction, and the government relied instead upon short-term bonds, establishing firmly that the government's solvency depended upon the renewal of these bonds and the goodwill of their holders. This was a dangerous practice: not only did it mean a very heavy short-term debt, but it mortgaged the life of a government to a small group of privileged persons, and at least twice during the interwar years a government of the Left was toppled because of the lack of confidence in it by the financial community. The budget was balanced by the device of a "special budget" composed entirely of reparations due from the Germans; when the Germans defaulted, the government had to borrow from its financial friends, and in 1923 believed it had to take action against Germany if any reparations at all were to be obtained. Thus there was no increase in taxation under the *Bloc National*, at least not until 1924, when taxes were raised 20 per cent in order to pay the collection fee for the reparations promised after the French occupation of the Ruhr.

Finally, while anti-Bolshevism provided an admirable cement for the *Bloc,* traditional conservative friendship for the Church led the government to seek what it described as "religious appeasement." This unhinged the *Bloc National,* which had included both clericals and anticlericals in 1919. If the canonization of Joan of Arc in 1920 could be accepted as a convenient marriage of patriotism and religion, resumption of diplomatic relations with the Vatican in 1921, the promise to exempt the recovered provinces of Alsace and Lorraine from the law on separation of Church and state and the laws curbing the Church's rights in education, and legislation permitting the Church to reoccupy its former properties, activated the latent anticlericalism of the Radicals, whose emotions told them that the Republic was once again threatened by clericalism. Much debate and passion on both sides were given to an issue long out of style. The Radicals were probably mistaken in their zeal. The governments of the *Bloc National* were hardly reactionary; not reaction but normality and quiet at home was their aim. Religious "appeasement" was meant to write finish to the quarrel of another generation; those who desired it simply underestimated the Radicals' capacity for self-deception.

The main business of the *Bloc National* was conducted in foreign affairs, especially from 1921 to 1924. The government, whether headed by Briand or Poincaré, had a quite natural obsession with security and reparations; the problem was could the former be had without abandoning the latter, and vice-versa? The French wanted both, and neither Premier could sacrifice reparations in order to obtain security—guarantees from the Germans that they would respect the other provisions of the Treaty, particularly the settlement of the frontier question—or sacrifice security, in this sense the enforcement of provisions limiting Germany's capacity for war, in order to obtain reparations. The inability to overcome this dilemma led to France's unilateral military action, the occupation of the Ruhr, in 1923.

Aristide Briand became Premier in January 1921, for the seventh time in his career. Later dubbed "the apostle of peace" for his apparent effort to achieve Franco-German rapprochement, Briand oscillated between firmness and flexibility toward the German problem. Since the Anglo-American guarantee given at Versailles was a dead letter, and faced with growing British suspicion of French intentions toward Germany, Briand initially pursued a tough policy, concluding a defensive alliance with Poland, thereby committing France to the role of policeman of the settlement of 1919. During negotiations over the sum of reparations due, Briand's government occupied the German cities of Düsseldorf, Duisburg, and Ruhrort, ostensibly to collect customs revenues. Reparations finally were fixed in April and May, and under threat of occupation of the Ruhr, Germany paid the first installment by borrowing in London. Of course it was going to be extremely difficult for Germany to pay the sum of 132 billion gold marks, and a breakdown in payments occurred shortly. After irritating the British by insisting that the Poles be given a share of Upper Silesia, despite a plebiscite in which the residents of the area voted for return to Germany, Briand took a turn toward leniency, and made discreet suggestions about the need for concessions. This so alarmed President Millerand and Poincaré that they undermined Briand in his own cabinet, and when Briand attended an international conference at Cannes at the end of the year, he was bombarded by missives from his cabinet demanding that he make no concessions, not admit the Soviets to the proceedings, and make no agreements without the participation of the United States. Briand understood very well what had happened, and resigned, without an adverse vote of the Chamber of Deputies, in January 1922. He had reached a dead end, although he had begun the creation, by alliance with Poland, of a system beset with danger, and had left the British irritated.

Millerand appointed former President Poincaré as new Premier. Poincaré's mental processes were now governed by an unyielding conviction that Germany must be made to honor her obligations, and with a government resting more narrowly upon the Right and Center, Poincaré's tactics, his repeated threats to employ force, and his determination created an atmosphere conducive to unilateral French action. Germany asked for a moratorium on her debt in July 1922, and when the German mark began to tumble wildly in October, Poincaré began to suspect that the Germans were not above going into bankruptcy on purpose so as to renege on payments. Seizing upon German nondelivery of certain materials, including telephone poles, Poincaré sent French troops into the Ruhr in January 1923. On its face, the operation was not especially successful, and it has generally been written off as a failure, a blind alley produced by French intransigence over reparations and giving France neither reparations nor security.

France was vigorously criticized by Great Britain, whose suspicion of French intentions bordered on the absurd and whose reluctance to involve herself in any continental squabble that might require Britain to fight was well known. Comforted by the British attitude, the Germans practiced passive resistance to the invader, and Berlin even hinted that it would pay the Ruhr workers not to work. Only after another smashing round in the decline of the mark, threatening the entire European financial system, did the Germans call off passive resistance and the French agreed to soften their demands upon the Ruhr mines. At this point Poincaré might have entered into an accord with German businessmen under which France might share in the products of German industry, or he might have given further encouragement to the Rhenish autonomous movement; either choice carried with it the risk of intense German resentment and desire for revenge. Instead Poincaré agreed to internationalize the issue and, after lengthy negotiation, the famous plan drawn up under the leadership of the American Charles Dawes provided for reorganization of the *Reichsbank* under Allied supervision, the rescheduling of reparations payments, and a loan to Germany. It could be argued that without the French invasion of the Ruhr that nothing at all would have been achieved: France could make more concessions after the invasion than before; the invasion forced Great Britain to act; and France finally was to receive reparations. Perhaps Poincaré's way was the only way for France to receive a measure of satisfaction. To much of the French public and the politicians of the Left, however, saddled with a 20 per cent rise in taxes to pay the costs of the Ruhr operation, Poincaré's magic seemed diminished if not fruitless, and the leftist victory in the election of 1924 was due, at least in part, to the widely held view that the invasion had been a costly mistake.

CARTEL INTERLUDE

In the legislative election of 1924 the *Cartel des Gauches*, composed of the Socialists, Radicals, and minor parties of the Left, won 328 seats, an apparent solid majority, to 226 seats for the parties of the Right and Center. Reasons for the triumph were several: by 1924 memory of *union sacrée* and fear of the "Red menace" had worn thin; the Radicals, apprehensive over the policy of the *Bloc National* toward the Church, had veered toward the Left, and made the clerical "threat" a major issue; Socialists and Radicals presented a common front in many departments, and their organizational ability worked to advantage; inflation had made deep inroads; the Ruhr invasion seemed to have been a poor investment; and the tax increase occasioned by the Ruhr occupation was less than popular. It looked as if a government of action had come to power, a government in the exact image of the "party of movement." But little over two years later, without benefit of a new election, Poincaré had returned to power, and the Cartel seemed broken. Splendid in their concern for symbolic acts, the governments of the Left accomplished little and appeared incapable of coherent management of the nation's affairs. Part of their failure was due to the intractability of the problems at hand and the tenacious defense of the privileged against any diminution of their privileges; a larger share of the failure is to be found in the Left itself. The period 1924–1926 was the first installment of three distressingly similar experiences; also victorious in the elections of 1932 and 1936, the Left could not withstand the test of power, and each time gave way within two years to the parties of the Center and Right. Much of the responsibility for this recurring fiasco lies with the Radicals.

It has already been observed that the Radical Party was the

almost perfect representation of the Republican synthesis, committed to the protection and defense of its heterogeneous clientele and thus to inaction under a splendid rhetorical cover. Radicalism was in part a state of mind galvanized at election time into a powerful political machine designed to capture votes. The Radical Party had something of a split personality, of a dual character, and was undermined by the running skirmish between its proclaimed ideals and the defensiveness of its politics. Hence at election time in 1924, 1932, 1936, and in some departments in 1928, Radicals aligned themselves with their neighbors on the Left, the Socialists; joint lists were presented in 1924, and in subsequent elections Radicals withdrew in favor of Socialists on the second ballot, and vice-versa, depending upon which stood best chance of election. But Socialist-Radical cooperation usually stalled shortly after the polls had closed, due partly to the Radicals' fear of the implications of their own leftist rhetoric, and Radicals drifted toward the Center and Right as it became clear that the price of cooperation with the Socialists would damage the pocketbooks of their clientele. When in working alliance with the Center and Right, called "concentration," Radicals soon became restless in their ideological confinement, and broke out of it by the time of the next election. Despairing of ever achieving a majority of the seats in the Chamber of Deputies, the Radicals were doomed to be the pivots of the political system and never its master. If the Radicals seemed in fact to have no real ideals or aspirations other than participating in power in order to protect provincial France against elderly enemies from the past and socialist dreams of social equality, they were men of government, a political class. Undoubtedly participation in political power was often an end in itself, and Radicals were past masters in the art of politics in the Chamber. Radicals were also men of talent; indeed the Cartel government of the great Radical leader Edouard Herriot in 1924 was viewed as the advent of "the Republic of Professors."

Socialists were not blameless in the failure of Cartel governments to accomplish very much and ultimately to endure very long. The postwar SFIO bore striking resemblance to the prewar model, although it was but a minority of the Socialist Party that had fought the election of 1919. After a period of internal upheaval, the Socialist Party had split at its congress of 1920 into a Communist Party with allegiance to the Third International of Moscow, and a group retaining the name SFIO. The Communist majority at the congress, as a political party, lived henceforth a life of turbulent negation, isolated from politics until 1934, and with a leadership increasingly in the image desired by the Kremlin, which followed the twists and turns of Soviet policy with remarkable fidelity.

The badly defeated minority was essentially the union of two minorities, one composed of the pacifist wing of the SFIO during the war, headed by Jean Longuet and Paul Faure, and the other, composed of those who had supported the *union sacrée* and an assortment of Socialist politicians, was led by Léon Blum, a former jurist and literary critic, an intimate of the assassinated leader Jean Jaurès, although he had entered active politics only in 1919. Blum's speech to the congress in defense of the principles of the "old house" was to become the cement and gospel of the reconstituted Socialist Party. Blum denounced Bolshevism as a narrow creed based upon its own peculiar experience and characterized it as a brutal departure from the traditions of European socialism. Bolshevism's errors, he thought, were staggering: it wrongly equated the seizure of political power with social revolution; its demand for dictatorial party organization was a thorough perversion of democracy; it threatened the independence of trade unions from party control, and it denied that workers could fight in defense of their nation. Because the majority of the congress, by voting to join the Third International, signalled that it willingly subscribed to these heresies, Blum and his supporters believed that they had no choice but to take leave of their former comrades and maintain a Socialist Party committed to the preservation of traditional socialist doctrines.

What Blum, who became the leader of the party, and Faure, who became its powerful general secretary, failed to understand was that traditional socialist doctrines were badly in need of repair or of untangling. Like Jean Jaurès, postwar Socialist leaders confidently awaited the completion of the French Revolution, hopefully through the rational persuasion of all Frenchmen that socialism was necessary. In short, Socialists would work for social reforms and for social revolution, preferably by the ballot box; but the possibility of violent revolution was never to be excluded. Collecting a clientele of lawyers, teachers, civil servants, and some workers, in large part from provincial France, the SFIO was still a party essentially committed to reform and to peaceful change; convinced that the prerevolution was to be of indefinite duration, it still wanted desperately to work within the framework of French democracy. But its revolutionary goal and its care for doctrinal purity often hamstrung its potential for real reforming activity. Its dilemma was cruel: could it share in the democratic process without abandoning the chance for revolution, or, by openly becoming a party of revolution, would it lose the possibility of achieving real reforms? Hence the SFIO took refuge in what seemed to be unintelligible doctrine governing its role in politics, while simultaneously becoming a large party with substantial representation in the Chamber of Deputies. Fearing participation in government under Radical tutelage, Socialists insisted that they would not participate unless they, not the Radicals, were the senior partners; they would, however, support a government led by the Radicals while preserving their full freedom of action. Such independence, of course, worried the Radicals, especially when the SFIO pegged its continuing support to enactment of legislation such as a levy upon capital. Given such a situation, Radical governments were inherently fragile.

The parties in opposition to the Cartel on the Center and Right were less parties than clusters of like-minded conservatives. As a general rule of thumb, the firmness of party organization declined in proportion to the place of a party on the political spectrum: the Communists on the extreme Left hoped to be monolithic; the Socialists were organized democratically, so

much so that major decisions could be made only by the representatives of the rank-and-file members; the Radicals' flabby
national organization, resting upon local committees of party
notables, was balanced by a central committee in Paris, which
set the rules for the Radicals in the Chamber; and the major
groupings in the Center and on the Right, the Left Republicans
(*Républicans de Gauche*)—a Center-Right party, despite its advertising—and the Democratic Republican Union (*Union Républicaine Démocratique*) pretended to be unified and organized
political parties only at election time. Thus the major figures of
the Center and Right—Millerand, Poincaré, and later André
Tardieu, Pierre Laval, Pierre-Etienne Flandin, and Paul Reynaud—were powerful political figures not because they led large
and disciplined parties, but because of their skill in parliament
and the confidence they inspired in the financial community.
Only Louis Marin, the leader of the URD, could be said to have
had a real political organization, and that was extremely frag-
mented; many of the URD deputies were members of families
that held their electoral districts as if they were hereditary fiefs,
like the Roulleaux-Dugages in the department of the Orne and
the de Grandmaisons in the Maine-et-Loire. It would be a mistake, then, to consider the political opponents of the Cartel to be
strong parties united in solid array. Their strength was due to
who they were, their parliamentary skill—especially in wooing
the Radicals—and to their friends on the outside of the political
arena, especially in business and finance. It should be added
that these men were firmly Republican; they had no quarrel
with the nature of the regime and no patience for the shrill
voices of the *Action Française,* still calling for the demolition of
the Republic.

The first Cartel government, headed by Herriot and composed of Radicals and their friends from splinter parties on the
Left, was given a pledge of Socialist support but not of complete
cooperation. To Herriot, achievement was measured in satisfying
gestures. Arguing that Millerand had exceeded the powers of his
office by his intervention in the electoral campaign, Herriot re-

fused to form a government until the President resigned, and Millerand withdrew. As soon as Millerand was evicted from the Elysée, the Presidential residence, a new occupant was elected by the National Assembly. In the election the votes of the Senators—themselves elected by a college of certain officeholders in each department, Senators were usually older and rather conservative political veterans—swung the balance in favor of a colorless and moderate Radical, Gaston Doumergue. Herriot also arranged for the removal of Jaurès's ashes to the Pantheon, France's hall of heroes, amid a moving ceremony comforting to the Socialists. As the capstone of his effort, Herriot sought to mold an anticlerical bloc with blustery talk about suppression of relations with the Vatican and of the exemption of Alsace-Lorraine from laws curbing the influence of the Church. The threats were not carried out, simply because the anticlerical issue fell flat. France was faced with tough financial problems, and the modes, rhetoric, and tactics of the past would not suffice to make them go away.

The illusion of action had to be replaced by the real thing. The financial burden created by short-term bonds, the occupation of the Ruhr, the needs of reconstruction, unbalanced budgets, and inflation—so severe that the franc had declined to 14 per cent of its 1914 purchasing power—made agreement upon a program necessary. The stumbling block was the absolute inability of the Cartel to produce a coherent financial program: Socialists insisted upon higher taxes on the rich, a capital levy, and other items noxious to the Radicals and frightening to the monied interests, who removed their funds to more hospitable places, preferably abroad, thereby drying up a source of short-term funds to the government. In such a state of incoherence, unable to satisfy his partners on the Left or the monied interests, Herriot was mercifully relieved of his burdens by defeat in the Senate early in 1925. Five more "Cartel" governments followed, each unable to extricate France from a deepening financial mire. Unable to produce a viable financial program, the Cartel collapsed in the summer of 1926, and the old magician, Raymond Poincaré, was recalled to service.

UNION NATIONALE

Poincaré was designated Premier in July 1926 and remained in office, bolstered by a substantial electoral victory in 1928, until forced to retire in July 1929 because of failing health. In the twilight of his political career Poincaré was immensely more successful than in his earlier career as President and Premier. Presiding over what became the most buoyant years of the interwar period, Poincaré won a measure of respect and trust unequalled by any other politician of the era. In part he was successful because he was thought to be indispensable, the only man with sufficient stature to appease most groups on the political spectrum and to inspire the public confidence which was a prerequisite to the reestablishment of healthy state finances, or, as was commonly said, "business interests entrusted Poincaré with the moneybags and the politicians confided the Republic to his care." No longer the partisan politician of the *Bloc National,* Poincaré issued an appeal for a wide *Union Nationale,* or National Union; men of the Left—Radicals and nearby groups— held the "political" portfolios in the cabinet (Interior, Agriculture, Public Instruction), men of the Right the "economic" portfolios (Public Works, Pensions), Poincaré himself was Minister of Finance, and Briand remained as Minister of Foreign Affairs. Poincaré's formula, to be sure, was a patchwork, but it was safe; it was the Republican synthesis at its smoothest, and, once again, the representatives of the working class were on the outside. Herriot and the Cartel had desperately needed a financial program; Poincaré at the outset needed nothing new. He practiced budgetary equilibrium, sought foreign loans, and then in 1928 effectively devalued the franc, making it more competitive in the world market although it officially lost four-fifths of its value. Poincaré had a quality unavailable to any other political figure: he gave Frenchmen a psychological confidence so strong that monies were enticed home from abroad, and benefitting from worldwide economic health and German recovery, Poincaré won the reputation as the restorer of France's finances, the "savior of the franc." No daring new programs, no great innovations; instead Poincaré meant stability, order, and peace. The election of 1928 represented a smashing vote of confidence in his ability to keep France locked in tranquility: 330 seats were won by the Center and Right, and with most of the Radicals in his camp until late 1928, Poincaré commanded 440 of the 607 seats in the Chamber.

If the name of Poincaré was synonymous with defense, the name of Briand was synonymous with peace; working in tandem, it was thought, Poincaré and Briand would ensure both defense and peace. Briand became something of a legend in his own lifetime, even among politicians. Like many members of the political class, he had begun his political career, as we have seen, on the extreme Left and had moved with almost indecent haste toward "respectability"; eleven times Premier, he held the post of Foreign Minister in sixteen different cabinets. He was known as a very crafty politician, who often gave preference to power over principle. Yet in his long tenure as Foreign Minister from 1925 to 1932 Briand achieved a remarkable reputation as "the man of peace" by his apparent efforts to win Franco-German rapprochement, make the League of Nations the working ideal that Wilson had intended, and to banish war from the lexicon of statecraft—as the fatuous Kellogg-Briand Treaty "outlawing" war attested. One should wonder if his policies were determined less by a surge of idealism than by circumstances, especially when he displayed no evident discomfort in serving under the man who had occupied the Ruhr.

The apparent failure of the Ruhr adventure was the starting point for Briand's policy; since force was ruled out, only conciliation might make Germany behave and Britain reliable. France simply had to break out of her isolation. The Locarno Treaty of 1925 was a vital first step: France and Germany mutually guaranteed the permanence of their frontiers with each other and with Belgium, and the agreement was itself guaranteed by Great Britain and Italy. The Treaty had obvious advantages to France: it settled the question of Alsace-Lorraine, presumably once and for all, ostensibly secured a British pledge to defend France, and created a spirit favorable to amelioration of Franco-German relations. Building on this spirit, Briand cultivated close relationships with Stresemann, the German Foreign Minister, and in 1926 France was a supporter of Germany's entrance into the League of Nations. In the League itself, Briand devoted many words to the ideal of collective security, and he found the League a splendid forum for his expressions of idealism. In 1929 Briand gave his consent to the Young Plan, which involved certain rectifications of reparations payments, and agreed to the complete withdrawal of Allied troops from the Rhineland, five years earlier than stipulated by the Treaty of Versailles. Late in 1929 Briand offered a scheme for a European federal union, which was never acted upon by the powers in question. Briand's foreign policy seemed imaginative and generous, and in large measure it was, but he and Poincaré did not neglect to take out insurance against failure.

The insurance was written in three parts: alliances, the League, and defensive preparations. Alliances with Poland and Czechoslovakia provided for military assistance in the event of German aggression, and added to France's commitment were alliances with Rumania and Yugoslavia. These alliances were meant to curb Germany's potential appetite in eastern and central Europe—an appetite real enough since Germany refused to acknowledge the permanence of her eastern frontiers as she had done with her western frontiers. On the other hand, the alliances cemented France's role as champion of the status quo and as the policeman of the settlement, thus raising German doubts about France's desire to be flexible. In the League, France actually was identifying her security with the security of the world, and collective security, as Briand saw it, was an instrument of coercion: was the League an organization for mutual discussions and accommodation, or was it a potential force to be employed against a single power? By endeavoring to make the League over into the latter, Briand was attempting to make it into the policeman of the settlement of Versailles, and this too detracted from the sincerity of his profession of peace and cooperation. Finally, in 1929 France began planning and construction of the famous Maginot Line, ranging along the length of the Franco-German frontier. Added insurance, perhaps, but unlikely to convince the Germans that the spirit of Locarno was the only bridge to the future. In sum, beneath all the fine talk, Briand was proposing a deal in which the Germans would waive their claims against the Treaty of Versailles in return for admission into the family of nations and relief from the economic pinch of reparations. France's alliances in eastern Europe, her conception of the League, and her new defense posture made it clear that she had not placed all of her confidence in the public vision of her Foreign Minister and that she had no intention of abandoning the main lines of the settlement of 1919. The nub of the problem, still unsettled when both Poincaré and Briand had left office, was that no German statesman could accept the Versailles verdict as final, and the strategies employed by the French throughout the 1920s refused to recognize that elementary fact.

4 / Tranquillity Lost, 1930-1935

Agriculture is the basis of France's riches.
GEORGES ROULLEAUX-DUGAGE,
DEPUTY FROM THE ORNE, 1932

[The events of] the sixth of February 1934 were a sinister attack against the Republic, and I ask myself how it could have failed; logically, it should have succeeded.
LÉON BLUM

When Raymond Poincaré passed the reins of power to André Tardieu in 1929 few would have suspected that the next half-decade would bring not a remodeled conservative liberalism but a staggering reversal in France's fortunes, a reversal that would be only a preview of things to come. Tardieu and his successor Pierre Laval found themselves faced with an economic crisis that they could neither control nor correct, and their Radical successors, victors in the election of 1932, could do no better. The year 1933 saw Adolf Hitler installed in Germany, and the soothing illusions fostered by Briand's policies were replaced by a frantic search for a viable policy toward Germany. By 1934 economic crisis, the problem of Hitler's Germany, and the obvious ineptitude of the politicians appeared to have provoked an impasse in the political system, if not the rupture of the Republican synthesis. The politics of safety came under sharp

49

assault from the politics of commitment; for the first time since 1919–1920 political matters seemed to be real and worth a struggle, and the great masses of Frenchmen involved themselves in politics with fervor and impatience. From the partisans of ideological revenge against the Republic to those tired of the ways of the "Republic of Pals," the times seemed to demand change, even a sweeping away of the political forms that had only recently worked so well. If some commentators are to be believed, the near victim of this coalescence of troubles and new political consciousness was the Republic itself, almost toppled on the wild night of the sixth of February 1934 when mobs surged against the police barricades guarding the Chamber of Deputies. Others have seen these events as an inchoate explosion of discontent, not a plot to bring down the regime. Whatever their intent, the demonstrators on the night of the sixth of February opened a period of tumult that was not brought to a close until 1937 or 1938. Before these events and their consequences are discussed, the economy and society in the interwar years must be examined.

ECONOMY AND SOCIETY

France's economic lethargy—in comparison to Great Britain, Japan, Germany, and the United States—kept alive her image as a nation of small shopkeepers and marginal producers. Subscribing to the ethic of quality workmanship done best by an individual or small production unit, Frenchmen refused to take any risks with the capitalist system, and were easily outdistanced by more dynamic nations. Whether these traits were owed to an aristocratic hangover, by way of an inherited repugnance for business, or to a refusal to expand out of fear of the social consequences, the fact is that in the period of greatest economic expansion—the 1920s—more Frenchmen worked in production units of two to five men (1,400,000) than in units employing more than 500 men (1,300,000). The following table demonstrates how slowly larger enterprises grew in France from 1906 to 1926.

Establishments employing	1906	1921	1926
2–5 persons	598,800	454,800	485,100
6–10 persons	55,000	56,600	69,700
11–100 persons	17,300	22,200	26,200
101–500 persons	3,900	4,900	5,900
more than 500 persons	611	716	953

Charles Kindleberger [1] has shown that it was not the lack of natural resources, labor supply, or capital that was responsible for France's relative economic backwardness. He has demonstrated that the faults were several and interlocking: the flow of capital was carefully controlled by prudent people, and often away from domestic investment; the family firm doggedly resisted market competition, and firms were reluctant to liquidate their competitors by ruthless competition; the family firm, passed on to each generation, was rarely excited by the prospects of innovation, preferring to maintain the practices of the past; "national character," or the insistence upon perfection instead of mass production; the fact that the masses were less interested in durable goods than in food and basic necessities; the compartmentalization of French society, which acted as a barrier to mutual stimulation and demand; an archaic marketing system; and the belief that government must protect and defend established interests rather than promote innovation (for example, virtually every deputy told his constituents that his first duty was "to defend the interests of our beloved region"—against everybody else, of course, and against change in general).

Against this background, the 1920s seem to present a different picture: industrial growth, the beginnings of technological advances applied to industry, and the elimination of some marginal producers appeared to indicate prospects for accelerated

[1] Charles P. Kindleberger, *Economic Growth in France and Britain, 1851–1950* (Cambridge, Mass., 1964), and "The Postwar Resurgence of the French Economy" in Stanley Hoffmann *et al.*, *In Search of France* (Cambridge, Mass., 1963).

change. The demands of the First World War created new industrial units, altered the economic geography of the country by shifting workers to new industrial centers, and the government intervened increasingly, if haphazardly, in economic matters. Some great captains of industry emerged from the war—Citroën, who had manufactured shells, and Loucheur, who had manufactured poison gas, and a good number of "war profiteers"—and were at the heart of the industrial expansion of the 1920s. Concentration of plants and of financial resources, new advertising techniques, intertwined directorships, financial holding companies, and rapid spurts in new key industries, like chemicals and electricity, developed in part by a keen interest in technological innovation, together spurred overall growth. The war, then, was an impetus to change; and accumulated unsatisfied needs from the war period, demands for construction and reconstruction, and the stimulation from inflation to produce gave the 1920s an undeniable dynamism. If the industrial production in 1911 equalled 100, then

$$1920 = 67$$
$$1924 = 118$$
$$1926 = 127$$
$$1930 = 133$$

On the other hand, such dynamism was relative to the immediate past, and France remained, as the earlier table indicates, a nation of small and intermediate enterprises. Industries were still scattered and some were in marked decline, such as cotton and silk; most were stubbornly resistant to structural change. In substance, there were too many producers and too many retailers to allow for a radical streamlining of production and distribution. The owners, to be sure, were better organized than ever before: the *patronat* (bosses), organized into the CGPF (*Confédération générale de la Production française*), represented a powerful arm of pressure and of defense; the famous *Comité des Forges* was a stern defender of the metallurgical interests; and the equally famous "200 families" retained their hegemony over the upper echelons of finance and industry. But the practice of short-term loans to the state adopted by the *Bloc National* and maintained by Poincaré meant that more and more fortunes were tied up in business with the state instead of in developing private industry, and thus became stagnant wealth. If some business organizations were remodeled in the 1920s, owners more prone to unite to defend and to innovate, and new financial groups able to marshal large amounts of capital were created, the overall result was not a second industrial revolution but a modest redirection of French industrial development.

The lasting impact of the world depression on France can be seen from these percentages of the growth and decline in industrial production in six major countries.

Country	1922–1929	1929–1937
Japan	+6.5	+3.6
Germany	+5.7	+2.8
France	+5.8	*−2.1*
Italy	+2.3	+1.9
United Kingdom	+2.7	+2.3
United States	+4.8	+0.1

France was the only country of the six to show an overall decline in the second period; in other words, France was the only country not to recover, in terms of production, from the depression by 1937. The depression was slow to hit France, and for a while her leaders thought that she was a healthy country in a sick world, and offered facile rationalizations, such as "small production units would escape the disaster" thanks to their owners' prudent refusal to engage in the kind of speculation that ruined Wall Street. Of course it was only a matter of a short time before France's markets began to dry up and thus decrease production at home; by 1932 production had fallen off 27 per cent from its 1930 level, and 260,000 were unemployed. Although Frenchmen escaped the massive unemployment that characterized depression America, few escaped hardship, and even in 1938 industrial production was inferior by 15 per cent to the 1928 level. Successive governments, as will be shown, had no solution other than cuts in spending and salaries, which gave no stimulation to a lagging economy. One result of the prolonged depression was the radicalization of workers and peasants, and the hostility of small businessmen, hit hard by the depression, to their demands.

French agricultural production was characterized by diversity in modes of proprietorship and exploitation, a low level of technical competence, and a nagging insistence upon individual rather than collective endeavors. Proprietorship varied from region to region: in some areas farming was done largely by agricultural laborers, who were usually worse off than the urban proletarians; in others, peasants rented land, and paid their rent in money or in kind, and share-cropping was still fairly common. In still others, independent peasant proprietors, owning their own land, squeezed out their existence by their own hands. The burden of the peasant, in almost all categories, was heavy: some were directly under the influence of the local *châtelain,* by custom and by habit, and his directives, whether political or economic, were followed with scrupulous care; the lands of most peasants were badly scattered, and much valuable time was lost in transit to and from them; most were too poor and too unwilling to invest in machinery—in 1922 there were only four departments (out of ninety) in which there were as many as fifty tractors per thousand farming units; and before the depression, peasants were atomized and still largely passive, refusing to work together, although rural cooperatives had made some headway.[2] The difficulties of peasant life were evidenced by the decline in active farmers: there were 8,770,000 in 1906 and 7,097,000 in 1936, and in 1931 the total urban population exceeded the rural population for the first time. The ravages of the World War—physical destruction of land and the loss of young farmers—are shown in these indices of agricultural production. If the year 1913 equalled 100, then

[2] Gordon Wright, *Rural Revolution in France: The Peasant in the Twentieth Century* (Stanford, 1964).

1919–1922 = 77
1923–1926 = 90
1927–1930 = 99
1931–1934 = 105

The peasant was not participating in the prosperity of the late 1920s. Prices to him were too high, especially with inflation, and he was selling too low. With the onset of the depression, matters became even worse; while his production increased from 1931 to 1934, his revenues dipped by 40 per cent. Little wonder that many peasants began to tire of pressuring their deputy to put controls on imports of foodstuffs and instead began to resort to direct action, and even to membership in peasant defense committees, a peasant political party, to a proto-fascist organization headed by Henri Dorgères, called, appropriately enough, the Green Shirts, and to Communist and Socialist peasant federations. The depression, in short, compelled the peasant to shake off his lethargy, to become vocal, and to organize. In the long run his effort represented the beginnings of modernization of agriculture; in the short run it contributed to the politicization of the countryside.

France in the 1920s and the 1930s was, and is today, many argue, a bourgeois country; the term "stalemated society" has been employed to describe a society in which middle-class values and beliefs—such as work and thrift—were the dominant values of a society in which mobility was the exception rather than the rule. Obviously there remained several layers to the bourgeoisie, ranging from the "200 families" at the top to the small shopkeepers and clerks at the bottom, and including civil servants, professionals, and countless other categories. Politically the bourgeoisie was united only on bare essentials—the need for a limited state to preserve the social status quo and to defend the clusters of interests upon which the political parties rested —and dispersed its political allegiance among parties ranging from the Radicals on the Left to the Republican and Democratic Union on the Right, although of course there were Communists, Socialists, and partisans of the *Action Française* who were from the middle classes. The bourgeoisie underwent a remarkable convalescence in the 1920s, as the old political system was revived, costly social reforms were avoided, and social revolution crushed in the bud in 1920, and prosperity apparently was a basic fact of life; when Poincaré saved the franc the rewards of the future seemed limitless.

In addition to their political hegemony, the middle classes enjoyed the security provided by their relative economic well-being; higher education, for example, was a bourgeois preserve. In the 1930s, however, comfort and satisfaction gradually gave way to their opposites as the depression led many middle-class people first to demand more protection from the state, for example, a rigorously balanced budget, deflationary economic policy, cuts in salaries, and then, in many cases, to overt disgust and despair with the state's inability to repair the economic crisis. Just as there was a marked tendency for the political radicalization of some elements of the peasantry, more often than not in the direction of the far Right, so elements of the bourgeoisie joined extraparliamentary groups, such as the *Croix de Feu*, allegedly a veterans' organization, out of frustration and anger—and fear. By 1936 many deputies who had formerly seen their task as "the protection of the interests of our beloved region" were making an overt and often radical appeal to the worst fears of their middle-class constituents; obviously these politicians had followed the fever chart of middle-class discontent with care.

Almost everyone knows that the French population remained stagnant during the interwar years, and in the years after 1935 deaths exceeded births. The population was becoming older, without the prospect of an immediate influx of young people; no wonder that talk of France's demographic inferiority to Germany was common, and that older people seemed to hold on to commanding positions in French society. The following table shows the very small increase in the population from 1921 to 1936 and the shift from the countryside to cities and towns.

Year	Population in millions	Urban (%)	Rural (%)
1921	39,2	18,2 (46.4)	21,0 (53.6)
1926	40,7	20,0 (49.1)	20,7 (50.9)
1931	41,8	21,4 (51.2)	20,4 (48.8)
1936	41,9	21,9 (52.4)	20,0 (47.6)

It would be a mistake to calculate from these figures that the majority of Frenchmen lived in large cities in 1936. In fact there were only seventeen cities with a population of at least 100,000 in 1936, and only one with over a million (Paris, with three million) and only two others (Marseilles, Lyons) with populations above 500,000. Fourth-ranked Bordeaux had only 260,-000. To be an urban dweller one had only to live in a very small town.

The quality of life for the average Frenchman, at least by modern standards, must have been very poor. The social pyramid and the beliefs upholding it, as described in Chapter One, remained much as before the war. This was still bourgeois France, where the worker remained isolated and concerned with making a living; in many ways, the conditions of his life had deteriorated. If the worker was guaranteed an eight-hour day by the law of 1919, he still labored six days a week, and in larger factories he was more alienated from his labor than before. In a country whose values insisted that the only worthwhile work was work well done by an individual, the parcelling out of labor into assigned and banal tasks was itself dehumanizing, and with the growth of middle-sized plants, the old tradition of collective work by a dozen or so workers on a project was cast aside. After the defeat of labor in 1919–1920, union organization lagged, and the CGT split into rival organizations, one sponsored and controlled by the Communists, the CGTU (*Confédération Générale du Travail Unitaire*); the CGT membership dipped to 400,000 in 1922, and was reconstituted slowly, and the CGT leadership, much less prone to adventure than before, acted with great caution. The prosperity of the late 1920s permitted general wage increases, but the workers were among the first to feel the severity of the depression. Although entrance into the bourgeoisie was perhaps more open than previously, it was a very difficult job for a man without the proper credentials. Education, theoretically democratic and open to all, provided the key to enter the bourgeoisie, but because of cultural deficiencies and the need to take a job, few sons of workers ever entered the university.

Leisure was afforded to very few. France produced 231,000 automobiles in 1930, and 165,000 in the depression year of 1935, but only in two departments were there as many as fifty automobiles for every thousand persons. Few people traveled; until paid vacations were stipulated by law in 1936, workers had no time to see their own country. Studies of rural towns show that most of their residents went to Paris once in a lifetime, if at all, unless they were migrating to what was thought to be the place of opportunity. Rural electrification proceeded slowly, and radios were not common outside of the towns. Small towns boasted of one or two motion picture theaters, but this entertainment was still in its infancy. Atomized by their values—the sanctification of family life, the nature of their work, and their fierce individualism—Frenchmen usually socialized at cafés; Frenchwomen remained at home and went to church. Frenchmen did read a lot, and most of the reading was of political content—cafés were often distinguished by the political orientation of their clients. The number of newspapers and periodicals published during the interwar years was absolutely astonishing: Paris alone had at least a hundred daily and weekly newspapers, and, as an example, the tiny department of the Cantal had sixteen weekly newspapers. Virtually all of these publications were, in one way or another, an arm of some group with political aspirations; *Le Temps*, the great Parisian daily, was the organ of financial circles and the Foreign Office, and every department had its own *La Croix*, whose contents ranged from banal religious news to wildly reactionary attacks on the world of the present. Every Frenchman could find a publication to his political liking, and if he could not, it seems that he started one of his own. The multitude of regular publications with overtly political content reflected the divisions of French society itself, and as the political situation became increasingly inflamed they became rallying points for political action.

NEW CONSERVATIVES AND OLD RACIALS

André Tardieu emerged as the preeminent political personality after the departure of Poincaré in November 1929. Tardieu was Premier until December 1930, not counting a brief interlude in February 1930, was the principal personality in the Laval government from January 1931 to February 1932, and returned as Premier from February to May 1932. A disciple and close friend of Georges Clemenceau, Tardieu had built his own formidable reputation as a journalist for the influential *Le Temps* and as an independent politician. He had figured in the negotiations at Versailles, and was known for his keen interest in foreign affairs and as a partisan of a hard line against Germany. His strength and weakness were in his personality: like Poincaré and Laval, he had no powerful political apparatus at his disposal; if he was supported by the parties of the Center and the Right, and if he was attacked passionately by the Left, his program clearly was borrowed from the Left. His very manner—impatient and haughty—and his authoritarian reflexes roused the hatred of the Left and the suspicions of his parliamentary majority; as one of his biographers has said "there was something provocative about his whole person." [3] He failed to accomplish very much at all, but he did intend to recast France and her political system after his own desires; in so doing, his effort constituted the first, but not decisive, break with the Republican synthesis.

Tardieu entered office with a call for reform and political concentration—meaning Radical participation in government with the Center and Right. The Radicals refused to join, and Tardieu was compelled to rely upon the conservatives for his majority; Briand, however, was kept on at the Foreign Office,

[3] Rudolph Binion, *Defeated Leaders* (New York, 1960).

more as a fixture than as a force, and he was quickly eclipsed by the new Premier. There was little question that Tardieu took power intending to use it, rather than simply to exercise it. He diagnosed the political system as one geared to noisy inaction, declaring that "it is as if the people were holding a perpetual election campaign and had given their representatives an imperious and permanent mandate to ambush any and every government." Almost immediately, Tardieu set out on a collision course with the politicians which ended with the victory of the latter and Tardieu's virtual severing, by 1936, of his allegiance to the parliamentary system.

In 1929–1930, however, he directed his attention to the modernization of France's economic structure, although such attention was not without consequences for the political and social structure of the country. The Premier proposed a "Five Year Plan," which some suspected to be an undesirable import from the Soviet Union in name and in content. It called for a great national effort for construction of homes, hospitals, roads, for rural electrification, the rationalization of industry (including the phasing out of outmoded plants), social and old age insurance, agricultural innovation, and for much else that was not only desirable but necessary. To ward off the depression, Tardieu proposed the investment of surplus funds into these programs, although full implementation would have required vastly increased state revenue. It was a remarkable program made by a remarkable man: it was the rudimentary blueprint for a welfare state. When the Left discovered that Tardieu had translated much of their blustery rhetoric into a program, they denounced him for theft, to which he retorted, "So you are going to shoot at me the very moment when I come before you bearing your children in my arms?"

The Left fired the traditional salvos reserved by the Third Republic for use against men of action. He was assailed as authoritarian, untrustworthy, and a budding dictator, and, with the exception of a broad social insurance scheme—for sickness, unemployment, and death, to be paid jointly by worker and employer—both Tardieu and his program were scuttled. Nominally defeated on a minor matter by the Senate in the fall of 1930, the reasons for his failure were several. He was the victim of the very appetites he had whetted, as the Left had to preserve for itself its claim to be the party of movement; how could the Left permit a man of the Right to carry out a leftist program without denying its own *raison d'être*? Conservatives naturally viewed his proposals with apprehension, if not fear; to them, Tardieu was doing too much too fast, and he left office supported by virtually no group. His proposals, if effected, could have spelled the doom of dear stagnant France: once modernization had gained momentum, it could have been uncontrollable. A placid bourgeoisie, outmoded industrial plant, archaic agriculture, and the beliefs justifying and praising all three, would have been called dramatically into question. Economic modernization, then, would have had political repercussions so severe as to undermine and perhaps to bring down the old political structure, the Republican synthesis. This is exactly what Tardieu had in mind. He desired to bring about conditions favorable to the emergence of a viable two-party system with parties free of antiquated ideological baggage and committed to practical action. Finally, the time was not opportune for such a program. What politician, before the debut of Keynesian economics, could have brought himself to vote for deficit spending in a period of economic depression? And Tardieu's proposals were financially very expensive. Although Tardieu accomplished little, his authoritarian manner, his proposals, and the kind of opposition that they aroused raised ideological tension to a pitch unknown since 1924. Tardieu had contributed to a polarizing of the Chamber into Left and Right, to a renewed consciousness of political division; in so doing his Premiership marked the first stage in the unraveling of the old political system.

After an ephemeral government headed by an ephemeral politician named Steeg, Pierre Laval arrived in power in January 1931 and was to stay for little over a year. Given his record in the 1940s and his execution for treason, one would expect that he would have been even more suspect than Tardieu (who occupied a prominent place in his cabinet). Such was not the case: a former Socialist with pacifist credentials, he had moved quickly toward the Right in the postwar years, had his slender political base in the Senate, and was unlikely to be an innovator in domestic affairs; in short, he was not regarded as a threat to the system. Moreover, his interest seemed pegged to foreign affairs, and while Tardieu's proposals lay dormant, Laval pursued an orthodox domestic policy (for example, the maintenance of a balanced budget and a careful watch on state expenditures). It was not until much later that Pierre Laval became the man determined to pull down the parliamentary system.

Like Tardieu, Laval found his majority on the Right and sought to lead it, in foreign policy, in directions not altogether of its choosing. Laval's unyielding fear of the Soviet Union and of the Communist contagion—he had made much political capital out of his anti-Communist posturing—and his hatred of war led him to seek amelioration of Franco-German relations. In 1931–1932 Laval trod a difficult path: the German government, mindful of the astonishing increase in Nazi strength, could make no meaningful concessions even had it the desire to do so; and Laval's own majority was not known for its patience toward Germany, especially over the ticklish question of reparations. Laval was hamstrung by the behavior of his supporters and the suspicion that his—and Tardieu's—actions aroused: in the first case, the Bank of France effectively vetoed the proposed customs union between Austria and Germany in 1931, raising serious doubts about Laval's protestations of goodwill; in the second case, Tardieu's proposals for an international police force and the gradual reduction of armaments were viewed as a shabby French effort to maintain arms superiority. Laval's interminable delay in agreeing to President Hoover's suggestion of a moratorium on reparations and interallied debts—which would have hurt France because she was due more in reparations than she was scheduled to pay to the United States—gave the Germans little comfort. Yet Laval persisted in speaking softly to the Germans, and even invited Chancellor Brüning to address the Chamber of Deputies, hoping that Brüning would forswear any effort to alter the Treaty of Versailles for ten years in return for unspecified concessions. No German politician could have made such a promise, and in January 1932, Brüning doomed Laval's government by declaring publicly that Germany would not pay reparations in the future. The government fell by vote of the Senate on another issue, but the clear failure of Laval in foreign affairs was the major factor in his defeat.

Given the disastrous impact of the depression and urgent internal and external needs, the inability of the Tardieu and Laval governments to do much of anything began to raise doubts in some minds about the viability of the existing political system, and the results of the election of 1932 transformed many of those doubts into certainties. An uninspiring political scenario became a low comedy tainted by scandal, and inertia seemed to be raised to the level of official policy. The election was similar to that of 1924: a *Cartel des gauches*, composed of Socialists, Radicals, and splinter groups, faced a *Union Nationale*, composed of the parties of the Center and Right. On the Left, electoral victory was their only sure reward since Socialists and Radicals practiced sufficient self-discipline to pool their resources on the second round; as in 1924 they could agree on little else save the need to win the election. The election was presided over by a caretaker government headed by André Tardieu, a significant fact only in that the President of the Republic, Paul Doumer, was assassinated between the first and second rounds of the election, and some have suggested that, given the panic and passions created by the assassination, Tardieu could have made himself dictator with a few telephone calls to the army and police; no one has demonstrated that Tardieu had any such intention or that he would have had such an easy job of it.

Tardieu scheduled a new presidential election—won by Albert Lebrun, the colorless and timid President of the Senate, the perfect man for presiding at flower exhibitions—and permitted the second ballot of the legislative election to take place without any disorder. The Cartel won 344 seats, and the Center and Right, 259. To demonstrate the multiplicity of groupings in the Chamber, here are the groupings, by their proper titles, and the number of deputies belonging to each, from Left to Right.

Communists	10
Workers' Unity	9
French Socialist Party and Republican Socialist Party	28
Socialist Party (SFIO)	131
Republican-Radical and Radical-Socialist (Radicals)	160
Radical Left	48
Independents of the Left	23
Independent Left	15
Republicans of the Left	29
Republican Center	34
Republicans of the Center	6
Popular Democrats	16
Republican Federation	41
Social and Republican Group	18
Independents for Economic, Social, and Peasant Action	7
Independents	14
Inscribed in no group	26

For twenty months, from June 1932 to the sixth of February 1934, Cartel governments struggled with their own incoherency. There were six governments, five of which were headed by Radicals—Herriot, Daladier, Sarraut, and Chautemps—and one by an ex-Socialist, Paul-Boncour. Their record was dismal by any standard, even that of the Republican synthesis. These governments were inherently fragile, because of lack of Socialist participation: Radical leaders simply refused to pay the Socialist ransom (for example, a forty-hour work week, nationalization of armaments industries) and the SFIO remained on the outside as sometime supporters. The Radicals simply could not sanction the interference in economic affairs that the Socialist demands would require; as has been said, Radicals may have defended the little man, but they were compromised by the big.[4] The only issue was an insoluble one, given the Radicals' unwillingness to commit themselves to economic and social innovation: how

[4] Peter J. Larmour, *The French Radical Party in the 1930's* (Stanford, 1964).

could governments carry out a deflationary economic policy, involving a balanced budget, cuts in expenditures, and cuts in the salaries of civil servants, who figured prominently among the clients of the Cartel? The answer was that they could not, and France lived for these twenty months in political stalemate. The first Cartel government, headed by Herriot, skirted the central issue, and rather than continue, Herriot chose a splendid way for his government to fall—over a principle. Herriot insisted that France should make her payment to the United States despite the lack of reparations from Germany, and he was soundly trounced by a vote of 402 to 187, with the Socialists voting against. Succeeding governments did no better, insisting as they did that there was no incompatibility between deflationary policies and continuing to seek help from the Socialists. Late in 1933, the rumor of a scandal involving prominent political personalities touched off an explosion, the events of the sixth of February 1934, which broke the political stalemate and perhaps also the Republican synthesis.

THE SIXTH OF FEBRUARY

The events of the sixth of February 1934 seem clear enough: right-wing gangs, united under the banners of several organizations bearing an alarming resemblance to Mussolini's squadrists and Hitler's storm troopers, massed across from the Chamber of Deputies in and around the Place de la Concorde with the apparent intention of invading the Chamber. Certainly the demonstrators were not friendly to the politicians: Edouard Herriot was struck as he left the Chamber and briefly surrounded by persons chanting "Into the Seine River with him." Herriot's misadventure was a testimony to his courage, since many deputies skulked out of the session as the chants of their potential assailants became louder and as the police fired into the ranks of the demonstrators, killing 14 and wounding 236. Barricades were erected by the demonstrators, buses were set afire, and sporadic shooting lasted into the small hours of the morning of the seventh, when finally the disorder expired. Premier Daladier, not a man to buck force for long, resigned, giving way to a basically conservative government of "national union," and the demonstrators seemed to have scored an initial triumph. If what happened on the long night of the sixth of February is now a matter of reasonably correct historical record, what the events meant is another matter.

On the Left, especially among the Socialists and some Radicals, the events were seen as a premeditated and coordinated assault against the Republic in the hope of installing a regime on the fascist model. Additional support for this view came in the years 1940–1944, when many of the same men who were active on the night of the sixth of February were either important figures in the Vichy regime or prominent among the collaborators eager to create a carbon copy of the Nazi regime in France. Partisans of the plot theory point to the marching instructions given to each of the participating groups, such as the *Action Française, Croix de Feu,* and the *Solidarité Française,* to the fierce anti-Republican campaign marshaled beforehand by the organs of these groups, notably the *Action Française,* and to the determination of the demonstrators to invade the Chamber of Deputies. As the Socialist chief Léon Blum later declared, the events of the sixth of February "were a sinister attack against the Republic," and "I ask myself how it could have failed; logically, it should have succeeded." Critics of the plot theory have argued that if the demonstrators were really serious about their business, they might have succeeded; as it was they were blunderers of the first rank, because any attempt to seize power should have included capture of key ministries, radio stations, telephone communications, and assurance of support or benevolent neutrality from the police and the army.

The idea of a plot against the Republic was largely a reaction of the first moment, although many who believed in it refused to be persuaded otherwise. Furthermore, they acted accordingly, setting in motion a general strike on the twelfth of February, a powerful demonstration of working-class strength and growing political consciousness, and this was followed by "unity of action" between Communists and Socialists in the summer of 1934 and the construction of a Popular Front, including Communists—who had been among the most vigorous critics of the Republic and who had taken to the streets to denounce it—Socialists, and Radicals in 1935 and 1936. In this series of events, antifascism was undeniably the motor force, grounded in a fear, at least at the outset, for the existence of the Republic itself.

Those who did the demonstrating disclaimed, in large part, any intention of replacing the regime with one fabricated in imitation of Hitler and Mussolini, and alleged that valiant patriots, who were exercising their right of protest against the politics of scandal and inaction, were brutally shot down on orders of a government that thus forfeited its right to exist. According to this interpretation it was the government that turned a demonstration into a riot, and then to shameful slaughter. Had a plot truly existed, according to the demonstrators, why were key ministries not assaulted, and why did Charles Maurras, potentially a leader of any insurrection, stay home in bed after having discharged his imperative duty by writing his newspaper article for the following day? Some have argued that the demonstrators did not desire to topple the regime, since Daladier's hasty exit from office and his replacement by a government clearly oriented toward the Right were sufficiently satisfying to them and there was no renewal of the demonstrations on the seventh.

Historians generally have rejected the plot theory, holding that the very incapacity and disorganization of the potential assassins of the Republic precluded the possibility that they were engaged in a frontal assault upon the regime. Likewise, the view that the fallen and wounded demonstrators were the hapless victims, indeed martyrs, of government savagery has not won much sympathy; clearly the demonstrators were not above performing their own acts of savagery, and the first shots may well have been fired from their ranks. Some historians have seen the events as a demonstration of protest against the regime which degenerated into a riot, thanks to the hotheads on both sides; others have argued that the intent of the demonstrators was to force a change of government, not of regime. Another view recently presented is that the events stemmed from a crisis of the regime, from the political stalemate of 1932–1934, and that only a "supercrisis" could break that stalemate. In other words, an outburst of intense dissatisfaction with the government's dismal record was perhaps inevitable and even desirable, in that it cleared the air, ended the Left's self-imposed paralysis over the financial question, and paved the way for the political alliance of the Left in the election of 1936. Finally, some have viewed the events as simply an effort by the new right-wing organizations to demonstrate their strength and vitality and to put themselves on the political map.

Perhaps all of these explanations possess, in differing degrees, enough validity to make them plausible, and taken together offer a more valid explanation than if taken separately. The immediate precipitants of the events are quite straightforward, and the fact that demonstrations against the government did develop should not have been surprising. Since the election of 1932 France had endured prolonged governmental inefficiency; whereas the Republican synthesis was geared to inaction, the lasting impact of the depression demanded action. Socialists wanted higher taxes on the rich and no cuts in state expenditures; the Center and Right—and their friends in finance —wanted a cut in state expenditures and reduction of salaries of civil servants; and the Radicals could not decide what to do. Since the Radicals were in power, this was an unfortunate predicament for them and a powerful irritant to the Center and Right. The growth of right-wing leagues, paramilitary organizations, the renewed vigor of the *Action Française*, and the development of fascist ideas and organizations (to be discussed below) were due in large part to the unedifying spectacle of a series of governments unable to deal with the critical problem of the moment.

The scandal that broke at the end of 1933, purportedly linking the dealings of a shabby financier named Stavisky in false municipal bonds in the city of Bayonne with several politicians, including a member of the Chautemps government, was a splendid opportunity for the several groups on the extreme

Right to denounce the government, especially when Stavisky conveniently killed himself as the police arrived at his door. Like the Panama scandal of almost a half-century before, the Stavisky scandal afforded the opposition its chance, but unlike Panama, the crisis over Stavisky broke in the streets and not in Parliament. The *Action Française* led a sharp attack by several newspapers on the Right against the government, and, under increasing pressure, Camille Chautemps gave way to Daladier, who, probably in order to win Socialist support, dismissed the tough Prefect of Police of Paris, Chiappe, who was extremely popular with the Right. The dismissal touched off the explosion of the sixth of February, although the dismissal was hardly a cause and was either the last straw or a great opportunity for the Right, particularly for the assorted groups comprising the extreme Right. The demonstrations were precisely that: only partly coordinated, their intent was to protest against the government, to bring it down if possible, and to display the strength of the new Right itself. Doubtless some were momentarily intoxicated with the thought of revolution, and had the police sided with the demonstrators, revolution might have been possible. But the fact remains that those who had for so long called for the destruction of the Republic—the *Action Française*—had made no plans for a seizure of power, and seemed astonished by their own strength. Force did win, since the government resigned in face of the events, but it was not the fascists or the leagues who were victorious. The winners were the conservative politicians of the Center and Right, who represented the center of gravity in the new government.

This is not to say that everything returned to normal and the French returned to politics as usual. In fact, the sixth of February 1934 stands out as the pivotal event of the decade, at least in internal affairs. Violence and direct action, once unleashed, acquire a self-sustaining dynamism of their own. The events of the sixth of February marked a decisive rupture with the Republican synthesis, a break that was not patched over until 1938, and then only temporarily. Politics became active, aggressive, participatory, and, for a time, polarized. The Left rallied to antifascism and Republican defense, and ultimately divided the nation yet further; the extreme Right, momentarily lulled by the conservative governments from February 1934 to January 1936, was to dream of, and to try to prepare for a real assault upon the Republic; and the politicians, by 1936, found that they were compelled, perhaps for the first time in their careers, to grasp an ideological banner and defend it with fervor.

FASCISM IN FRANCE

It is extremely difficult to deal with French fascism, for it scarcely existed; it existed more as a fear that it inspired than as the reality it was.[5] On the night of the sixth of February there was no fascist party worthy of the name, and it was not until 1936 that a real fascist party was born, the French Popular Party headed by an ex-Communist, Jacques Doriot. Even then Doriot was not without challenge and competition from ideological kin operating as parties, groups, movements, and as individuals uncommitted to any organization. In France as elsewhere fascism was a convulsive and self-advertised revolutionary repudiation of political liberalism, a force of protest against the alleged decadence and paralysis of the nation, and a call for heroism and action. Fascism as a mentality undoubtedly had more influence in France than as a party or even a doctrine, and as such it attracted some of the best young minds, such as the writers Robert Brasillach, Maurice Bardèche, Drieu la Rochelle, the literary critic Thierry Maulnier, and the political scientist Bertrand de Jouvenel. Fascists together engaged in a desperate and often violent search for the renewal of their nation, but, more often than not, their effort was little more than a romantic flight into unreality. Their record is written in division and failure, at least in the 1930s; it was not until the Republic was defeated on the battlefield and buried at Vichy in July 1940

[5] See Robert J. Soucy, "The Nature of Fascism in France," in Nathanael Greene, ed., *Fascism: An Anthology* (New York, 1968).

that fascism was to have a real opportunity to attempt to install itself in France.

Like fascists elsewhere in Europe at the same time, French fascists enlisted under the banner of order, authority, and nation, and dreamed of total revolution against what they thought to be total decadence. Like other fascisms, French fascism was entangled in its own confusions and paradoxes: partisans of order, fascists themselves provoked disorder and exalted violence as the release of creative human energy; while aspiring to be a mass movement basing its power upon popular approval, fascists cultivated a narrow elitism, believing that only a few were fit to rule; calling for heroic action was easier than practicing it; and the rhetoric of revolution masked an unyielding fear of dramatic social change. Even more than elsewhere doctrine was secondary: French fascists delighted in the sheer romanticism of action; their business was to shock, to destroy the idols and myths of liberalism by attacking capitalism and by vilifying parliamentarianism as the regime of hacks, and by portraying themselves as a virile force of refusal. They cultivated assiduously the activist mystique, redemptive myths about the open air, sport, and physical courage, and engaged in much heady talk about the creation of a new human type. Many of them persuaded themselves that they were the pilgrims of a new Europe, a fascist Europe, and they rejoiced in the apparent solidarity of international fascism. Indeed many attacked the lifeless nationalism of their mentors, especially the old men of the *Action Française,* and sought to place themselves outside of traditional nationalism. At the time of the Spanish Civil War some of them found their heroes in the cadets of the Alcazar of Toledo, who resisted the siege of the Republican forces, and at the battlefields of Madrid. In short, they were the wave of the future, but unhappily, heroism could only be found beyond French frontiers, a problem that was to cause them considerable inconvenience when France was faced with the threat of German aggression in 1938 and after. Could French fascists accept the annihilation of their nation as the ransom for the final victory of fascism? Confronted with this dilemma, French fascists were virtually helpless in their effort to control events.

Reasons for the emergence of French fascism are not difficult to uncover; indeed it would have been very surprising had such a movement not appeared in a nation with a long history of counterrevolutionary movements and doctrines and with the Bonapartist tradition—order, authority, and the promise of social appeasement—and with a regime never fully accepted by all. In a Europe in ferment, where authoritarian regimes of surface dynamism and vitality seemed to be the norm and democracy the exception, small wonder that the vagaries of the Republican synthesis should repel many active and young people; the conviction that their nation was sunk in decadence and decline was the cementing belief of French fascists. The response of the Left to the events of the sixth of February, the formation of the Popular Front, the Socialist-led government headed by a Jewish Premier in 1936, social turmoil, marked by a wave of occupations of factories in 1936, and the mushroom-like growth of the Communist Party, all contributed to the building of a sharp reaction against the alleged leftist threat, which many interpreted as a threat of social revolution on the Bolshevik model.

In part French fascism was a reaction against the middle-aged and elderly reactionaries who had for so long held proprietorship of the counterrevolutionary tradition, and even Charles Maurras was not immune from harsh criticism from rebellious former pupils. French fascism was also the rejection of the conservatism, personified by Poincaré and Tardieu, that had fully accepted the Republic and had worked within its institutional framework. French fascism was ultimately the product, not the initiator, of crisis at several levels—political, economic, social, diplomatic, and intellectual. Crisis was the handmaiden of fascism, without which it could not have developed and without the perpetuation of which it could not have survived.

A singular characteristic of French fascism, as compared with other branches of the fascist family, was its extreme diversity, its multiplicity of organizations, and its inability to produce a single leader. Excluding the paramilitary leagues, such as the

Croix de Feu, led by Colonel de la Rocque, which were more pressure groups of excitable war veterans than fascist organizations, and the *Action Française*, whose ideology remained steadfast and whose organization showed the strains of age, there existed a generous handful of groups anxious to retool the Right in its own image, such as the Young Patriots (*Jeunesses Patriotes*); *Francistes;* French Solidarity (*Solidarité Française*); the Green Shirts, an effort to create a peasant fascism headed by a fiery demagogue, Henri Dorgères; the Hooded Ones (*Cagoule*), a murder club; the Insurgent (*L'Insurgé*), headed by Thierry Maulnier; Doriot's French Popular Party (*Parti Populaire Français*), among others. Despite the diversity, the themes were fundamentally the same, from the movement of the 1920s headed by Georges Valois to the party of Jacques Doriot. Valois, financially supported by the perfumer Coty, as were several other overtly fascist groups, issued a call to combat against what he described as the Slavic hordes of Bolsheviks and appealed for a single nationwide party, a single leader, and the organization of the nation by professions and families. His fascist legions, the "Blue Guards" briefly recruited well among veterans and the discontented petty bourgeoisie, but both Valois and his organization faded away when Tardieu came to power.

Marcel Bucard, leader of the small *Franciste* organization, expressed the aspirations of fascists when he declared: "Our parents wanted liberty; we demand order. They preached fraternity; we demand discipline. They professed equality; we affirm a hierarchy of values." French fascism conceived of itself as the personification of youthful dynamism, and its enthusiasts emphasized the gulf between generations, contrasting the sham of the Republic, associated with older people, with the vitality of fascism, portrayed as an invention of youth, and fascism's appeal to the young is undeniable. Drieu la Rochelle summarized this sentiment very well: "To live audaciously and with strength is, today, to be a fascist! Everything that is moving and active in this world is fascist." And Jacques Doriot summarized the essence of the fascist message thus: "Our youth have the right to say that we have not bequeathed to them a very glorious page of our history. Our politicians still speak the same language, still repeat the same clichés. They employ thirty-year-old slogans . . . To save our country from decadence, an end must be put to this incoherence; we must give France a unity of command, a unity of action . . . The French Popular Party must be a fighter and a hero."

A major barrier to fascist success in France was, obviously, the very incoherence of those who denounced the incoherence of the Republic. How could so many organizations, movements, and groups, armed with a potpourri of very general themes and often given to romantic fancies, hope to persuade many Frenchmen that they were the wave of the future? Commitment to revolt was one thing, but ability to shape events quite another. Yet there were several other factors in the failure of French fascism to be a serious alternative to the Third Republic. Fascism came to power in Italy, and Nazism in Germany, because of the confluence of certain conditions, most of which were absent in France. Both Italy and Germany suffered from nagging national frustrations, and Germany from defeat in war and at the peace table, whereas France was largely exempt from such feelings. Economic crisis produced widespread despair in Italy and Germany and a momentary consensus that remedies could not be found through existing channels; the depression was not as devastating in France, and arguments were over what weapons to use to combat it, deflation or modest innovation. If France's political system appeared to be faltering, France had, unlike Germany and Italy, a venerable democratic tradition, and in Germany and Italy the old conservative political class boosted the fascists to power, but most French conservatives—at least until 1940—maintained their allegiance to Republican institutions. In Italy, and especially in Germany, fascism appealed to the discontented of all classes, especially the frightened middle classes, and profited from the fragmentation of society; France had built-in safeguards against fascism in her tightly structured society, the traditions of the family and individualism, and the bourgeois beliefs that buttressed the "stalemated" society.

In short, there were too many people who had too much

to lose by participating in movements that advertised their commitment to overturn almost everything. In Italy and Germany, fascism triumphed in part because of the weaknesses of parties of the Left, who marched divided to their own annihilation; the French Left forged an antifascist coalition that endured until 1937 or 1938, by which time the Republican synthesis was sufficiently repaired and able to withstand every shock but military defeat of the nation. There were other factors in the fascist failure: suspicion of the Bonapartist tradition, which meant dictatorship; the general fidelity of the army and police to the Republic; and, it should be repeated, the inability of French fascism to produce either a single leader or a great mass movement. Finally, it could be argued that French fascism was born too late in history; while it built upon the French counterrevolutionary tradition and had some of the opportunities available to Italian and German fascists, it could not escape the accusation of being a shabby imitation of foreign models and, ultimately, against the nation. A fundamental contradiction undermined French fascism from the start: could one admire Hitler and still be for France? A great many admirers of fascism chose for France.

"CINCINNATUS" AND HIS SUCCESSORS

When Daladier fled from power on February 7, 1934, the elderly ex-President of the Republic, Gaston Doumergue, a nominal Radical with a pronounced inclination toward the Center and Right, was recalled to service, this time as Premier of a government of "national union," a shadowy euphemism for a government oriented toward the Right of the political spectrum, although it included Radicals. Doumergue likened himself to the Roman Cincinnatus, who was called from his farm to assume the powers of the state in time of crisis; the Left remembered that Cincinnatus had been a dictator, and issued the appropriate warnings. The Left need not have been so apprehensive: Doumergue had always been an outstanding mediocrity, and he would disappoint no one now. Doumergue did have one vital asset—he was a Republican who stood for the existing Republic, and, thanks to his conservative credentials, his presence at the helm of government dampened the agitation against the regime. Doumergue had no readily discernible program except praise for his own presence, although he talked about the need for "authoritative government," evidently at the prompting of his Minister of State, André Tardieu. Time and his own political miscalculation worked against Doumergue: the passage of time eased the threat of a new crisis, and Doumergue became less and less needed; and Doumergue made the fatal mistake of desiring to alter the political system. Doumergue acted scandalously in the eyes of many politicians by addressing the nation by radio in a number of "fireside chats" in which he castigated the Left, describing socialism and communism as twin brothers. His charges were less serious than his act: a Premier simply did not speak over the heads of the parliamentarians to the people. In his efforts to secure more authority for the government, Doumergue proposed reform of the electoral system to eliminate the second round, which had been advantageous to the Left, and asked for a virtual free hand until May 1935. This was too much for the Radicals, who withdrew from the government despite Doumergue's alleged threat of street demonstrations in his behalf. His bluff called, "Cincinnatus" retired to his farm for the last time.

Doumergue was succeeded first by Pierre-Etienne Flandin, a bland Center politician, whose apparent determination to apply the brakes to the deflationary policy and to expand the availability of credit was undermined by the Bank of France, a private institution, and he was replaced in June 1935 by Pierre Laval. Laval was to hold on to power until he was dumped by the Radicals in January 1936. Both governments were based upon "concentration," that is, alliance of the Radicals with parties to their right. In too many ways, 1935 was the year of Laval. As Foreign Minister under Flandin and in his own government, his actions contributed to exacerbate tensions at home. His insistence upon a frankly conservative financial policy—deflation accompanied by decree laws slashing state salaries, described by the Left as "decree laws of misery" [6]—as well as his evident indifference to the growth and pugnacity of the paramilitary organizations, contributed significantly to the increasing polarization of public opinion. In Paris on the fourteenth of July, the anniversary of the taking of the Bastille in 1789, the *Croix de Feu* marched on the Champs-Elysées, while the Left marched in another and less elegant part of the city; in Algiers thirty planes allegedly belonging to the *Croix de Feu* flew menacingly over the city. The shaping of the Left into the Popular Front will be discussed in the following chapter; it is sufficient to note that the rise in tension and the sense that a confrontation was in the offing was in no way alleviated by Laval's actions. Essentially it was the way Laval "debased everything by fixing, intrigue, and slickness," as Léon Blum put it, that aroused much hostility and passion. Nowhere was this more evident than in Laval's foreign policy.

Laval's foreign policy marked a transitory phase in the evolution of the Right and Center away from a firm, sometimes harsh policy toward Germany in the direction of what later became known as appeasement, although it was not until 1936 that their social fears—dread of the "Red Menace" at home and abroad—began to outweigh their traditional anti-German inclinations and lead some of them to the rationalization that Hitler was a bulwark against the spread of communism. Interestingly, the Left began in 1934 to move precisely in the opposite direction, away from pacifism and generosity with regard to Germany toward a firm opposition to Hitler. Changes in attitude of such magnitude did not occur all at once, or at a steady pace, or without uncertainty and confusion. Laval's foreign policy exemplified this perfectly: the purpose of his machinations was obscure, perhaps even to himself, and it may be that he was playing both ends against the middle in the hope that something positive would result. Were his efforts aimed at winning Franco-German

[6] Decree laws were promulgated by the government by virtue of prior authorization from Parliament; in other words, the government was given a blank check to do as it saw fit in a particular area.

rapprochement, or were they aimed at building a formidable alliance against Hitler?

Taking over the Foreign Ministry after the assassination in 1934 of Louis Barthou, who had attempted to tighten France's ties with her friends in eastern Europe and who may have considered alliance with the Soviets, Laval centered his attention upon the Italian dictator, Mussolini. A recent biographer of Laval [7] has argued that his overtures to Rome were designed to provide a link to Germany, and this was Laval's main aspiration. But it should be remembered that Italy and Germany were not the partners in 1935 that they were in 1938, and that they were separated by key issues, among them Germany's apparent designs upon Austria; in fact, Laval, Mussolini, and MacDonald, the British Prime Minister—all of them ex-Socialists—met at Stresa in April and vowed to maintain the settlement of 1919. Another view is that Laval was seeking Mussolini's cooperation in an effort to keep Germany isolated. In either case Laval was not very successful. By giving Mussolini what the *Duce* thought to be a blank check to move against hapless Ethiopia, Laval mortally weakened the League of Nations; when Italy launched her aggressive war against Ethiopia, the League had to respond with sanctions against the aggressor, but their meager application, especially by France, finished off the League as an instrument of collective security. The *Duce,* moreover, was not especially pleased to find that his adventure did not have the support that he had anticipated from Paris, and France's image was sullied by her association with a fascist dictatorship, especially in the eyes of the Left, whose spokesmen denounced Laval for flirting with fascism.

The famous and abortive Hoare-Laval Pact, agreed upon at the end of 1935, made matters even worse: Laval and the British Foreign Minister agreed upon terms of a settlement of the Ethiopian affair that were very favorable to Italy, and their premature disclosure in the press let loose a flood of outrage,

[7] Geoffrey Warner, *Pierre Laval and the Eclipse of France, 1931–1945* (New York, 1968).

especially in Britain, which resulted in Hoare's hasty resignation. The British government pretended that Hoare had been led astray by the wily Laval, and Franco-British relations suffered appreciably.

Laval had compiled a dismal record: he had not won over Italy, for whatever purpose; he had helped to create an estrangement between Paris and London; and his negotiation of the Franco-Soviet Pact, providing for mutual assistance but without a binding military convention, was unlikely to win Hitler's friendship. Laval's own doubts about his pact with Stalin led him to postpone its ratification; and it was not ratified until after his departure from office (Stalin was unlikely to view Laval's government as a partner against any German threat). Thus Laval had worked at cross-purposes and had succeeded in undermining the League of Nations and in irritating the British, Mussolini, Hitler, and Stalin. This was a formidable record of failure in foreign relations. And at home, Laval's activities contributed to widening the growing division of the nation.

5 / A Nation Divided, 1936–1937

> You will vote, citizens, either for the Popular Front, with all its horrors—revolution, war, state socialism, monopolies, and suppression of private property—or for the Party of Order, grouping together all Frenchmen having a common doctrine, the worship of the fatherland.
>
> GASTON MOREAU,
> DEPUTY FROM THE MAINE-ET-LOIRE, 1936

> We want to resurrect hope, we want to fight against poverty, we want France to regain confidence; and we want to live in peace with all nations of the world, whatever the internal policy of their regimes. War is possible only when one believes it to be possible; inevitable when one proclaims it to be inevitable. I refuse to despair of peace, and of the action of the French nation for the preservation of peace.
>
> PREMIER LÉON BLUM, 1936

> For the first time, this old Gallic-Roman country will be governed by a Jew.
>
> XAVIER VALLAT,
> DEPUTY FROM THE ARDÈCHE, 1936

The Popular Front was born in reaction to the apparent threat of fascism in 1934, attained its maturity in the hectic year 1936, and died a lingering death in 1937 and 1938. For some it was a great adventure, for others a great fear; few Frenchmen could afford to be indifferent to it. The year 1936 was a time for commitment, for mass involvement, for action, and for the attraction of extreme remedies for France's ailments, real and imaginary. In short, it seemed to be the time to choose sides— against other Frenchmen—while calling for national unity of purpose. Political parties and extraparliamentary political groups, unions, big business, the Church, and countless other groups and sectors of French society, especially youth, involved themselves in what some thought to be an ideological struggle that transcended the ordinary run of politics, social divisions, and diplomatic maneuverings. To join a party or an organization, to take to the streets with banners and song, or to occupy a fac- tory was to signal one's participation in change or in defense of values and possessions under assault. For a brief historical mo- ment, a wave of ideological contagion swept across the nation, touching not just Paris but the remotest regions and villages; something really new and different seemed to be happening, something destined to sweep away the Republican synthesis and to replace it with a dynamic regime of the Left or of the Right. Doubtless some had a dream or a nightmare of revolution, even if no organization canalized whatever revolutionary energy that may have existed, although some did try. Appearance was more certain than reality, but only briefly; by the summer of 1937, if not before, the popular fever had lowered appreciably, the old politicians had reoccupied center stage, and "normality" had been recaptured. What some had thought to be an opening to the future turned out to be only a brief interlude of excitement and agitation that had produced some changes in the national life, and much bitterness and division.

Legend, of course, dies hard and is often more appealing than fact. The legend of the Popular Front as a great and spontaneous upsurge of the masses is more attractive than the real Popular Front, which was basically an unstable political alliance of temporary duration. Mass action certainly did play an important role, but it never was the main story. Moreover, the Popular Front was not just an episode in domestic politics, although purely domestic issues—the threat of fascism, the de- mands for social changes, the need for economic revival, and the quest for the fulfillment of France's democratic promise—were at its origin and involved much of its career. The Popular Front was also bound up with international affairs, especially with the problem of Hitler's Germany. In retrospect, foreign policy questions may have been as influential in shaping the development and determining the life of the Popular Front as domestic questions. The impact of the Spanish Civil War did much to undermine the Popular Front while it created sharp and emotional divisions among Frenchmen, to the point that Premier Blum may have feared a civil war in his own country. When Spaniards fell to slaughtering one another, and when the totalitarian powers—Germany, Italy, and the Soviet Union—assisted them in their task, the specter of war, international, civil, or both, seemed real enough. It would be no exaggeration to say that by the end of the summer of 1936, foreign affairs had eclipsed domestic squabbles as the major concern of Frenchmen.

The Popular Front was, and remains, controversial, and it is only in very recent years that historians have begun to approach it with the skills and disinterestedness of their trade. The Popular Front was many things: an instinctive reflex against internal fascism, and thus negative and defensive; an enlarged Cartel, foredoomed to the fate of earlier Cartel models; "an entirely new experience in French history," as Léon Blum put it; a French "new deal"; a revolutionary impulse that expired thanks to the Communists, who exhibited a dread of revolution; a foreign policy ploy of the Soviet Union; and a profound effort to revive the national will to shape France's own destiny. Many on the Right were persuaded that the Popular Front was intended to be a prelude to Communist revolution, and cast Blum in the role of the hapless Kerensky whose Russian Provisional Government was overthrown by the Bolsheviks in 1917; many of them also viewed any effort at social amelioration as tantamount to revolution. The Right was also helplessly suspicious of the Popular Front's aims in foreign affairs, and some of its spokesmen never tired of denouncing the Popular Front for allegedly wanting ideological war against Nazi Germany. After the defeat of 1940, many of these same spokesmen accused the Popular Front of having paved the way for the disaster by dividing the nation, crippling her army, and even for allegedly rejecting the possibility of Mussolini's help against Hitler.

On the extreme Left, the failure of the Popular Front was its failure to lead a revolution when everything was possible; Communists, by their subservience to Moscow, which allegedly sought bourgeois France as a military ally against Hitler, and Socialists, hampered by their adherence to legality and by their timidity, were, in this view, responsible for the *révolution manquée*. Some historians, while admitting that the Popular Front created more emotion than accomplishment, consider its contribution to have been the spirit of renewal that later characterized the Resistance during the Second World War. These views, and many more, comprise the dossier on the Popular Front. The Popular Front was many things; for a time its existence polarized the nation, although sharp lines of division ran through all groups, parties, and sectors of society. In substance, it was an effort at renewal, by democratic methods, of a tired nation faced with multiple problems, but it was an effort restricted by circumstances, by the renewers themselves, and by factors over which Frenchmen could have little control.

THE LEFT REBORN

The genesis of the Popular Front is to be found in the reaction of much of the proletariat and some of its leaders to the events of the sixth of February 1934. Communist and Socialist leaders found themselves compelled to associate in a vast general strike on the twelfth of February in protest against the "fascist" plot against the Republic, but, despite clamor for closer cooperation between Socialists and Communists from excitable left-wing Socialists, both parties continued to hurl invective at each other until the summer, when the Communists abruptly made significant concessions to the SFIO. The result was a "unity of action pact" between the two parties, and although they did little but promise not to injure each other and collaborate in a minor way, the pact was a significant step toward unity on the Left.

A second stage in the development of the Popular Front was

led by the Communists, who began to direct friendly signals toward the Radicals and the CGT and warned of the need for a wide popular movement to crush fascism in the bud. The second stage reached its emotional peak on the fourteenth of July 1935, when Daladier, Blum, and the Communist leader Maurice Thorez marched arm in arm through the streets of Paris, and together with a vast throng took an oath to "remain united to defend democracy, to disarm and dissolve the seditious leagues," and "to give bread to the workers, work to youth, and a great humane peace to the world." The Congress of the Radical Party, meeting in October, in a fit of Republican and antifascist zeal, voted to join a great effort to "defend the Republican regime and public liberties" and called for the construction of a common program by the parties that had participated in the "grandiose popular demonstration of 14 July."

The third stage consisted in negotiations among Radicals, Socialists, and Communists, and these concluded in January 1936 with the announcement of a common program. Rather than specific demands, such as structural reforms of the economy as suggested by the SFIO—which gave the impression of so much foot-dragging—the Communists and Radicals insisted upon a program of splendid generalities in order to win wide popular support. Ultimately the program of the *Rassemblement Populaire*, as it was called, was subscribed to by some ninety-eight organizations, including such unlikely groups as the *Ligue des Bleus de Normandie, Union naturiste de France,* and the *Amis des Fêtes du Peuple.* Under the headings "Defense of Liberty," "Defense of Peace," "Against Unemployment and the Industrial Crisis," the program promised that its signatories would rid France of fascism, work for world peace, and restore economic health; in substance it was a declaration of many good intentions. Later the three major parties agreed to present a united front on the second round of the election, much as Socialists and Radicals had done in the election of 1932. It should be asked why each of the three parties—Communists, Socialists, and Radicals—adhered to the Popular Front and what each expected of it; such inquiry may well reveal the inherent fragility of the enterprise they had undertaken.

The decision of the Communists to make an armistice with the Socialists and then to take the initiative to form a Popular Front represented a hasty and almost indecent about-face. Since the Congress of Tours in 1920 Communists had been confined in large part by their own choice, to a political ghetto, from where they issued intransigent verbal assaults on just about everyone and everything. Once purged of undesirable and unreliable elements, the Communist Party had followed the twists and turns of Comintern policy with canine-like fidelity: Socialists were baptized social-fascists and combated as tools of the bourgeoisie, and the Republic, as late as the sixth of February 1934, was designated an enemy to be crushed. Despite the allegiance of certain intellectuals to the Communist cause and pockets of strength among the industrial proletariat, the party remained essentially isolated, lagging behind the Socialists in popular appeal, evidenced by the election of 1932 in which the SFIO outpolled the Communists by almost three to one. The Communists did have strength in their organization, were capable of loud campaigns of ideological annoyance, and were the beneficiaries of the chronic protest vote, but little else. Yet by 1936 the Communists had become a vast popular party, doubling their 1932 vote in the election of 1936, increasing their appeal markedly in the unions, and integrating themselves, at least temporarily, into the political system; all this because they were able to seize upon a key issue at the key moment by discarding the rhetoric of the past and grafting a new ideology onto an already existing organization. The issue was antifascism, the moment was dominated by a fear of fascism and for the Republic, and the ideology was patriotism and movement, or Jacobinism refurbished.[1]

Essentially the Communists adopted a defensive and decidedly nonrevolutionary posture, proclaiming that the times demanded the defense of the Republic and its liberties, unity

[1] See Daniel R. Brower, *The New Jacobins* (Ithaca, N.Y., 1968).

against the threat of international fascism, and certain modest social improvements. Vaulting over the Socialists, Communists extended the hand of friendship, as they put it, to the Radicals and later to virtually all elements on the political spectrum, even to Catholics, insisting all the while that social revolution was in abeyance for some time to come. Formerly partisans of revolutionary defeatism, a position that held that the workers had no country, would fight for none, and if war should erupt, would attempt to strike down their own government, Communists overnight became patriots, supported budgets for national defense, vowed that the worker would defend his country, gave the tricolor flag equal prominence with the red banner, and sang the *Marseillaise*, the national anthem, as much as the *Internationale*. Communists formerly had denounced all alliances as causes of imperialist war; especially after the signing of the Franco-Soviet Pact in 1935, they clamored for alliances to curb the danger presented by Hitlerian Germany. In sum, Communists were attempting to persuade potential allies and the French public that they were both necessary and safe: necessary to any successful defense of the Republic, but not any threat to it or to bourgeois society. Their task was difficult, for they often frightened those whom they wooed and terrified the conservatives, who began to envisage a Communist takeover in France.

The explanations for this apparently bizarre behavior are not difficult to uncover. By 1934, international communism had an almost unblemished record of failure behind it: undiluted hostility to the Socialists and democratic liberals had not only isolated the Communists and diminished their effectiveness, but had produced disaster in Germany. For a time Communists had held the insane view that Hitler's accession to power would represent a step toward Communist revolution, since Hitler represented the last gasp of a dying bourgeoisie. By 1934, Communists were disabused of their illusions; Hitler's Germany was not about to erupt into red revolution, and it posed a grave threat to the security of the Soviet Union. Hence an effort by Moscow to break out of her own isolation was natural and inevitable, and many historians have argued that the Popular Front was designed to make France a reliable military ally of the Soviets by insuring that the workers would be anxious to defend the U.S.S.R. against Hitler and by assuring "bourgeois" France that Communists were reliable partners in defense against fascism at home and abroad. Communists also were to stimulate antifascism in France and prod the French government to take a stiff line against Nazi Germany, preventing at all costs the nightmare of an isolated Soviet Union facing a powerful Germany.

Most historians suspect, given the unavailability of Soviet documents, that the Soviets were attempting to build a preventive alliance against Hitler, but others have argued that Stalin was simply attempting to build credit in the West and to prevent a possible alliance of Britain, France, and Germany against the U.S.S.R. with the intention of betraying his would-be allies at a critical moment by striking a bargain with Hitler, as Stalin did in 1939. Some have stated the view, which was a widely held suspicion in the 1930s, that Stalin was attempting to promote a conflagration between Germany on the one hand and France and Britain on the other, a war so exhausting to the combatants that the Soviet Union could step in and establish her sway over the ruins of old Europe. Whatever Stalin's intentions—and it is probable that he had chosen no one course, but was creating as many options for himself as possible—the French Communists were operating basically as agents in the foreign policy interests of the Soviet Union. Doubtless the policies pursued after the sixth of February also worked to the decided advantage of communism in France: the Communists emerged from political isolation, won a large following, could influence governmental policies for the first time, and created for themselves the mystique of being the antifascist party par excellence. At the same time, however, the Communists' freedom of action was circumscribed by the goals set down by Moscow: Communists could not be revolutionary and were compelled to downgrade social reforms in order to be able to influence the "bourgeois" parties to stand firm against Hitler. Communists would soon discover that they were the prisoners of their own limited aspirations.

Having rid their party of unpalatable and undisciplined in-

dividuals, some of whom had flirted openly with fascism, Socialists entered the Popular Front with surface enthusiasm and
unity.[2] Enthusiasm and unity, however, were ambiguous qualities
for the SFIO, whose theories and practices had not been appreciably updated since 1920. The SFIO was the political home of
men with potentially conflicting views, particularly over international policy and the reliability of the Communists as a force
for peace. Diversity may be tolerable in a period of stability; in
the crisis situation of the 1930s it was a fatal flaw. The majority
of the party, comprising the Socialist deputies and senators, and
the bulk of the rank and file in departments where socialism was
an entrenched and powerful political force, found its spokesman
in Léon Blum, leader of the parliamentary contingent and direc-
tor of the Socialist daily, the *Populaire*, and Paul Faure, General
Secretary of the party. Both men had been the architects and di-
rectors of Socialist policy since the Congress of Tours, a policy
that had combined intermittent collaboration with the Radicals
with efforts at social amelioration by legislation while insisting
upon the final goal of social revolution.

Blum and Faure often spoke with contrasting voices, but
declined to perceive the contrast. Blum, gentle, humanitarian,
and confident that the unfolding of French history would ultimately bring revolution, was anxious to participate in the Popular
Front. Faure, political tactician, organizer, and ardent polem-
icist, had grave doubts about entangling alliances, especially
with the Communists, whom he regarded with unremitting suspicion. This divergence in temperament and views carried over
into foreign affairs. Both spoke in the language of pacifism about
the need for international understanding, disarmament, and the
horrors of war, but with the arrival of Hitler in power, Blum
reluctantly moved away from pacifism toward the recognition
that force might be the only response to the new Germany, although he never publicly abandoned the vocabulary of pacifism.
Faure held fast to his pacifist commitment, refusing to consider

[2] See Nathanael Greene, *Crisis and Decline: The French Socialist Party in
the Popular Front Era* (Ithaca, N.Y., 1969).

the employ of force in international affairs, save to defend France if she should be the victim of unprovoked aggression, and he increasingly regarded the Communist attempt to galvanize opposition to Hitler as a plot to throw Europe into a war from which only the U.S.S.R. could hope to profit. Blum and Faure tried to speak in harmony, and often succeeded in doing so, but the increase in international tension in the years 1936–1938 ultimately led them to a public split, which ruined the SFIO as a viable political party.

The SFIO also had a vocal left-wing, which gained many fresh recruits in the exciting atmosphere of the Popular Front. The Left, like the majority, was also divided, essentially into two camps. One, led by a combative civil servant, Jean Zyromski, subordinated revolution and pacifism to the need to defend the Soviet Union, and his views were often indistinguishable from those of the Communists; like the Communists, Zyromski became the prisoner of his limited aspirations. The second, identified with a popular militant schoolteacher, Marceau Pivert, displayed confidence in the imminence of revolution, an example of their proficiency in the art of escaping from reality. Such confidence permitted the "Pivertistes" to view the Popular Front as the opening act of the revolution and to denounce any sort of preparation for a possible conflict with Germany as akin to fascism itself. Given such diversity, and the real possibility that it would blossom into sharp division under the strain of events, it is surprising that the SFIO was able to appear as unified as it did.

Appearance, however, was persuasive. To the public and to much of the SFIO, Léon Blum was the unquestioned spokesman for the Socialist and Republican ideals, and his own conception of the Popular Front was ratified by the party as its official position. It would be erroneous to assume that Blum's conception of the Popular Front was wholly defensive and even negative; he considered it to be an entirely new phenomenon in French history, a "current and an organization of forces which, until this moment, did not exist." He believed that its task was heavy. The Popular Front must render France immune to the disease of fascism by a vigorous assertion of the "Republican spirit" and by the defense and elaboration of democratic liberties. France, by her very example, would revive Europe's confidence in herself, thus facilitating the construction of a real system of collective security. Economic distress, which Blum attributed to the "absurdities and inequities" of capitalism would be met by state intervention at the "nerve center of the economic body." In essence a Popular Front government would be a government of the public good whose primary objective would be the moral and material regeneration of France, and thus of all Europe. As such it would be obliged to restrict itself to the confines of "Republican legality"; as it would owe its existence to the majority of the nation and not to one class, so it must fulfil its contract with that majority.

For Blum the Popular Front was not a revolutionary movement, not a simple defense against fascism, nor was it to be the guardian of bourgeois society; its mission was the salvation of the nation. He warned his party that the task would require time, patience, order, and caution; force would be unnecessary because the old order was already crumbling beneath its inner contradictions, and dangerous because it would create panic and disorder, weakening France in a time of peril. Socialism's vocation to transform society would remain unalterable, but the party must realize that the fate of the nation itself was at stake. As for himself, he asked his party "if I have the qualities of a leader"; he responded that he did not know. Could a man so intensely humanist, who abhorred war and violence with genuine passion, have the will to act with firmness, even with ruthlessness? Blum thought that he knew what must be done; time would prove that he would be unable to do it.

Past performance should have been an accurate gauge of Radical behavior in the Popular Front: torn between their leftist impulses and rhetoric on the one hand, and their concern for their pocketbooks on the other, Radicals had not been very reliable partners in the Cartel experiences of 1924–1926 and 1932–1934. Radicals, in their majority, adhered to the Popular Front almost by reflex, from the imperative of Republican defense, and from the assumption of electoral reward. Edouard

Daladier emerged as the unlikely champion of the Popular Front in Radical ranks in 1935, and like the Radicals themselves, the "Bull of the Vaucluse," as he was fondly called, was a weak reed upon which to rely; he would be the gravedigger of the Popular Front in 1938. A few Radicals, very few, were enthusiastic about alliance with both Communists and Socialists; a majority gave it their temporary blessing and approval; and a large minority, preferring the comfortable tactics of concentration, worked to undermine and embarrass the Popular Front almost from the start. Precious little idealism was involved in the Radical choice; for most Radicals, electoral advantage, the opportunity to govern, the defense of the Republic, and the prospect of a number of modest reforms were the determining factors. The Radicals were never so enthusiastic about the Popular Front as at the beginning; by 1937 most of them were anxious to extricate themselves from what had become to them an annoying and even dangerous alliance.

As noted, many organizations and curious groups adhered to the Popular Front. One of the most important was the CGT, reunited with the Communist-led CGTU early in 1936 under the impetus of the Popular Front atmosphere. The CGT, still under the leadership of the crusty, veteran unionist Léon Jouhaux, for whom the defeat of labor in 1920 and the subsequent years of union weakness were still a living reality, was anxious to pursue a policy of caution. Reforming legislation, to ensure a forty-hour week and paid vacations, was the target of the Jouhaux unionists; revolution was out of the question. Once unity of the ranks of labor had been reestablished, Jouhaux was very concerned with keeping order in his own house by smothering differences and emphasizing the virtues of agreement over limited aims, thus preserving the CGT from the ravages of ideological fever. There was, however, a definite potential for internal disruption within the reunified CGT. Communist unions from the former CGTU were unlikely to abandon their former allegiance; unions in which Socialists predominated, such as the teachers' union, shared the outlook and suspicions of Paul Faure in the SFIO; and no one counted on the vast influx of recruits to the CGT, many of whom joined out of a commitment to revolution. If the Popular Front stimulated the unions to unite once again into a single organization, the very excitement that it created spelled trouble for those who wanted only reform.

The Popular Front also found active and articulate champions among intellectuals, and in a country where intellectual achievement was highly regarded such support was valuable beyond the boundaries of the intellectual community. If fascism, with its promises of action, change, and dynamism, attracted prominent writers and critics, so the Popular Front offered a similar attraction; in a way the division of intellectuals mirrored the division of the nation itself.

As early as 1932, the renowned writers Henri Barbusse and Romain Rolland launched a "world movement against war" at Amsterdam, and in 1933 an impressive gathering at the Salle Pleyel in Paris formed the so-called Amsterdam-Pleyel movement. Although it was well populated with Communist sympathizers, Amsterdam-Pleyel represented an initial effort at union of left-wing intellectuals against fascism. Later in 1933 a group organized by Professor Langevin, the ex-Radical Gaston Bergery, and the Communist writer Jean-Richard Bloch, sought to mobilize a "common front" to study and combat the fascist menace, and although premature—the SFIO forbade its members to join —it helped to prepare the groundwork for the movement that was created in 1934 and 1935. The "Vigilance Committee of Anti-Fascist Intellectuals," formed in 1934 by Langevin, Paul Rivet, and the Radical philosopher Alain, won 8,532 adherents by mid-1935, representing a powerful force of opinion pushing for unity on the Left. Important periodicals, such as *Marianne,* *Vendredi* (directed by André Chamson and Jean Guehénno, and featuring contributions by André Gide, Romain Rolland, Roger Martin du Gard, and Aragon, the literary giants of the interwar years), and *La Lumière* were ardent antagonists to the right-wing periodicals *Candide, Je Suis Partout,* and *Gringoire;* verbal injuries were hurled in a reciprocal rhythm of increasing violence. Just as the Communist Party took the leadership in mobil-

izing the political Left, Communist intellectuals took the initiative
in mobilizing intellectuals of the Left. The intellectual climate
itself favored engagement in politics: one need only mention
Malraux, Saint-Exupéry, and Gide to demonstrate the vogue of
commitment to a search for meaning in life, a search often identified with action and the romanticizing of action as an end in itself.
The need for comradeship and struggle, for collective adventure
against the apparent stagnation and purposelessness of life, were
constant themes among intellectuals who flocked to the struggle
against fascism; ironically, much the same could be said of
those who adopted the fascist mantle as their own.[3]

THE POPULAR FRONT IN THE ELECTION—
AND IN THE FACTORIES

An apparently unavoidable feature of elections everywhere,
and especially in France, is shrill rhetoric and dire predictions of
what one's opponent will do once elected, predictions conveniently and necessarily abandoned once the polls have closed so
that government can work. Even given this standard, the election of 1936 was remarkable for its viciousness, almost to the
point of being a verbal civil war between two well-defined camps
who refused to perform the customary graces after the votes
were in. Actually the Left was much more restrained than its
opponents, calling for defense against fascism and promising
no more than the implementation of the Popular Front program;
even the Communists took great care to persuade the voters that
they did not want social revolution, but desired only a "strong,
free, and happy France." Speaking for the SFIO, Léon Blum
reaffirmed the ideals of socialism, and issued a plea for help in
"the highest and most noble work that some men can propose to
other men"; neither class war nor class vengeance figured in his
appeal. The Radicals employed rich rhetoric, pointing up the need

---

[3] See H. Stuart Hughes, *The Obstructed Path* (New York, 1968), and
David Caute, *Communism and French Intellectuals* (London, 1964).

for greater equality, and declared that their aim was nothing short of a "new order" created, of course, within the framework of liberty.

Nonetheless, the conservatives were frightened, and permitted their social fears to outrun their good sense. The violence of the Right was largely confined to words, although a cowardly assault upon Léon Blum in February by *Action Française* hooligans sharply raised tempers on the Left and created much sympathy for the Socialist leader. But the words of the Right betrayed their fear: the instructions of an obscure deputy, Gaston Moreau, to his constituents, warning of "revolution, war, state socialism, and suppression of private property" if the Popular Front should be victorious, were common in the conservative camp. Casting a wary eye at Spain, where the election of a Popular Front in February 1936 inaugurated a wave of violence that was to culminate in civil war, conservative spokesmen like Henri de Kérillis freely predicted identical ruin and disaster for France in the event of a left-wing victory at the polls. For a brief moment it looked as if French conservatives might be preparing to emulate the dismal record of their ideological cousins, the conservatives in Italy and Germany, who boosted dictators to power out of fear of a nonexistent threat of social revolution, although French conservatives had neither a candidate nor a party that could perform the job.

The results of the first round of the balloting confirmed preelection forecasts of a Popular Front victory, but aside from the astonishing success of the Communist Party, which increased its popular vote by some 700,000 over its 1932 total, and the spectacular decline of the Radicals, who sustained a loss of 400,000 votes and saw their share of the electorate dip from 20 per cent in 1932 to 16.5 per cent, the most remarkable feature of the first round was the relative stability of public opinion. The major parties of the Popular Front increased their total share of the vote by a mere 1.5 per cent, while the percentage of the parties of the Right and Center dipped slightly. The Socialist vote, by comparison with 1932, was a model of stability: the party gained a slim 32,000 votes, and its share of the vote dropped almost imperceptibly from 17.1 per cent to 16.9 per cent. What had occurred was a reshuffling of the leftist electorate, a sharp swing in its center of gravity toward the Left: Communist gain, Socialist stagnation, and Radical loss was the electoral balance sheet of the Popular Front formula.

The second round fulfilled the trends of the first: Communists won 72 seats, a gain of 62; Socialists won 146, a gain of 16; and Radicals won 115, a loss of 43. The ability of the Popular Front alliance to hold firm during the second round—coalescence of the Left around a single candidate, usually the one who had received the highest vote among left-wing candidates—spelled a victory of apparently considerable proportions, although many Radical voters marked their ballots in favor of candidates of the Center and Right rather than vote for a Socialist and especially for a Communist. On paper, the Popular Front majority in the Chamber was impressive: 378 seats to 236 for the Center and Right. However, one need only subtract 115 Radicals from the Popular Front and add them to the Center and Right, producing a new majority, 351 to 263. Given the previous behavior of the Radicals, the aspirations of the Communists, and the internal division of the Socialists, the Popular Front majority was immensely more precarious than the figures suggest.

As soon as the results of the election were known, the Socialists, having the largest single bloc of seats in the Chamber, feverishly declared their intention to head a Popular Front government, and Blum and Faure invited their electoral partners and the CGT to share the burden of power. The Communists, surprised that Socialists had elected more deputies than the Radicals—whom they had been flattering for almost a year—refused Blum's offer, arguing lamely that their presence in the government would serve as a pretext for unnamed "enemies of the people" to foment disorder, and their chief, Maurice Thorez, offered Blum only meaningless platitudes. Nonparticipation put the Communists in a splendid tactical position: they could claim generous accolades for their apparent support, but had hands free to browbeat the government. The Radicals, anxious for office as always, accepted, but intimate discussion between Blum and the testy leader of the CGT, Léon Jouhaux, failed to undermine the old unionist's disdain for politics and politicians, and the CGT declined the invitation. Thus the Popular Front government was composed essentially of Socialists and Radicals.

Scarcely installed, the government headed by Léon Blum—the first Socialist and the first Jew to be Premier—was confronted with a double-edged crisis that threatened to topple it and to throw the country into chaos. Class warfare seemed to be a sudden and appalling reality: occupation of the factories by the workers, much in the same fashion as in May 1968, spread contagiously across the country, while a frenzied flight from the franc threatened the Treasury with a massive loss of gold. The twin aspects of the crisis were due to anxieties and expectations generated by the Popular Front victory. The working class, suddenly aware of its muscle, impatiently demanded the rewards promised by the Popular Front; "we want to give Blum a push," said a factory worker in Paris. The moneyed groups, apprehensive that the new government would institute control over the exchange of currencies or devalue the franc, hastened to transfer massive sums to more hospitable places, such as Switzerland; this was the same tactic that had helped bring down the Cartel government of Herriot in 1925. Because Blum had widely advertised his commitment to speed France's convalescence from the depression, he was faced with the awkward task of reassuring both workers and financiers without antagonizing either irreparably.

The most dangerous aspect of the crisis was the wave of sit-in strikes: millions of workers occupied their factories, brought in food, drink, and bands, and had a fine time, escaping from the dull routine of their lives. The mood was that of a holiday, not of a revolution. But the fact that workers, spontaneously and on their own initiative, were sufficiently politicized to undertake such a movement was very alarming in the context of 1936. Communists were worried, since their instructions called for a strong France and not a France torn by social tumult and even by revolution; Radicals began to feel decidedly uneasy over what they had helped to create; and Léon Blum could see his vision of the Popular Front slipping away by the hour. The conservative President of the Republic, Albert Lebrun, exhibiting his tendency to panic at times of tension, literally begged Blum to soothe the workers with whatever promises were necessary. Obligingly, Blum took to the radio and declared that the government would be responsive to the workers' just demands. At the same time, Blum warned that order must be maintained, although he was unwilling to employ the full force of the state to evacuate the factories, explaining that recourse to police action could have produced outright civil war. How armed forces could evict millions of workers and then get the factories running was something that Blum's critics failed to consider when they decried his weakness in the face of illegal action.

Fortunately for the new government, and unfortunately for the few revolutionaries who began to think that the long-awaited moment to topple capitalism had arrived, the conclusion of the so-called Matignon Agreements (negotiated at the Hôtel Matignon, the Premier's official residence), wrenched from the representatives of a frightened *patronat*, conceding the right of collective bargaining and granting a general wage increase; and the rapid enactment of accompanying legislation by Parliament guaranteeing a forty-hour work week, paid vacations, and collective bargaining, plus the energetic intervention of Maurice Thorez urging a return to work, assuaged the temper of the strikers. By the end of June 1936, the unrest had largely faded, and the government could congratulate itself for its resolution of the crisis.

Successful in launching a program of social reform—including the creation of a Wheat Office charged with overseeing the production and distribution of wheat—and firm in its role as guardian of "Republican legality" (demonstrated by the dissolution of the leagues, such as the *Croix de Feu*), the government failed in its effort to revive France's lagging economy and to liquidate the financial chaos. Blum selected Vincent Auriol, a veteran Socialist politician and longtime party spokesman on financial matters, to be his Minister of Finance. Auriol was firm only in knowing what he was not going to do, and he based his financial policies on uncertain assumptions that proved to be an unhappy choice. Both Blum and Auriol initially refused to consider a devaluation of the franc, which was overvalued in terms of the world market. For political reasons they could not maintain the deflationary policies of their predecessors. Instead they pursued a policy that was grounded in the assumption that increases in salaries, plus an expanded program of public expenditure, would combine to yield a vast increase in the purchasing power of the population, thereby increasing the level of consumption, which in turn would stimulate production and economic recovery. This would provide additional state revenue, and permit the maintenance of the hallowed balanced budget. Ideally, workers would have more money and business more sales, and thus holders of capital-in-exile would be willing to invest in the French economy. Obviously, it was hardly a Socialist scheme.

Unfortunately, the government's expectations proved to be illusory, and for several reasons: (1) the government's reform of the Bank of France, taking it out of private hands and making it a public enterprise, did not help allay the suspicions of the financial community; (2) the franc remained overvalued; (3) the social legislation raised the costs of production; (4) the cash increments received by the masses were apparently spent on basic commodities, such as foodstuffs. Thus, increased spending failed to stimulate an increase in industrial production, and public expenditure increased budgetary disequilibrium. Although the flight from the franc slackened early in the summer, the gold reserve was vulnerable to a resumption of the exodus without warning. Moreover, the government believed that it could not institute control over the exchange of currencies because of the hostility of its Popular Front partners to any measure remotely resembling a structural reform of the economy. The financial problem was to return to constitute a permanent harassment to the government, and eventually was a source of its collapse.

IN SEARCH OF PEACE

Foreign affairs came to occupy a much larger place in the life of the Popular Front than anyone would have anticipated at its inception, and the domestic impact of events beyond the French frontiers, especially the Spanish Civil War that erupted in mid-July 1936, perceptively altered the concerns and the nature of the Popular Front itself. By the end of August, the Popular Front was out of phase: created out of fear of a threat to the Republic, it had to deal with the passions and anxieties generated among its opponents as well as within its own precarious ranks when external affairs took precedence over domestic concerns.

Léon Blum took office with a renewed confidence in his ideals and in France's ability to bring about the pacification of Europe. As he repeated many times, "war is possible only when one believes it to be possible; inevitable when one proclaims it to be inevitable. I refuse to despair of peace, and of the action of the French nation for the preservation of peace." Blum made ringing appeals to international conscience and morality and held fast to his conviction that disarmament was the necessary prerequisite to Europe's moral regeneration. However, these beliefs were tempered by the nagging reminder that the so-called pacific powers must be resolved to prevent a recurrence of armed aggression. To this end Blum honestly sought to repair France's good credit with Great Britain, sorely damaged by Laval's machinations and by Britain's behavior in the Rhineland crisis of March 1936, when the caretaker government of Albert Sarraut believed that France could not move against Hitler's military reoccupation of the Rhineland without positive signs of support from London, which were not forthcoming. Thus France had made no riposte at all, permitting the Führer to smash another provision of the Versailles Treaty. Blum's emphasis lay not on force, but upon the voluntary cooperation of all nations, regardless of their political regimes.

Regrettably, any detailed inquiry into the foreign policy

pursued by the Blum government would show that Blum's international policy was inherently dualistic, sometimes even contradictory, and painfully naive. Wise statesmen generally seek to maintain a generous supply of alternatives, but Blum was well stocked with illusions, giving him the unlimited right of expectation. In effect Blum believed that France could afford the luxury of noncommitment to any policy that carried the risk of her irrevocable estrangement from Germany, and partly as a result, he worked at cross-purposes. He devoted much energy—discussions with an emissary of the Führer and many fine speeches —and hope to an effort to alleviate tension between France and Germany, and he combined affirmation of France's pacific "mission" with emotional pleas for general disarmament. Yet Blum shunned contact with Mussolini, for reasons not fully understood, and publicized expenditures for increased French armaments. Willing to sacrifice pride and independence in an effort to cement ties with London—especially over the war in Spain—Blum refused to reinforce the Franco-Soviet Pact with a binding military convention, which may have undermined the credibility of France's commitments in eastern Europe. Blum later was to claim that, by 1936, he had concluded that binding military alliances were the only means of security for France. Actually his policy in 1936 and 1937 was still in flux. Blum clung to a lingering optimism that goodwill and reason were the stuff of diplomacy; armaments and alliances were meant not to intimidate, but to persuade, and were insurance against failure. At the same time, Blum continued to employ the generous rhetoric of pacifist idealism. "Socialism," he declared, "incarnates the struggle against war, incarnates the will to extirpate the roots of war from the human mind." And he sincerely believed what he said.

The Spanish Civil War was, without question, the most serious crisis that Blum was to face. Basically the war comprised two issues for France: (1) it was directly involved with her relations with all major powers of Europe; and (2) it was a domestic issue that accentuated the polarization between Left and Right, at least at the outset. When the war erupted, after the failure of the uprising of the Spanish generals to seize all of Spain had touched off a violent social revolution in several parts of the country, the Spanish government addressed an appeal to the French government asking that it be permitted to purchase arms from France to be employed against the insurgent generals. Blum initially was favorable to the Spanish request, which violated no international agreement, and was himself very sympathetic to the Popular Front government in Madrid. Very shortly, however, the civil war in Spain threatened to become an international imbroglio, as Italy and Germany hastened to aid the cause of the sedition, and the Soviet Union, and its mouthpiece in France, the Communist Party, demanded aid to the forces of the Spanish Republic.

Many people, including highly placed officials in London, believed that the war in Spain could ignite a general European conflagration, and the British government was extremely anxious to avoid this possibility. Many French officials, especially among the Radicals and some Socialists, were of the same opinion. On the Right—one of whose members had expressed his hatred of Blum by declaring to Blum's face "this old Gallic-Roman country will be governed by a Jew"—opinion was nearly unanimous in support of the Spanish generals, who were portrayed as Christian saviors fighting against the scourge of communism. Opinion was quickly and fiercely mobilized in France for each of the camps fighting in Spain, although only a minority of the Left, Communists and certain Socialists, favored selling arms to the Spanish Republic, which carried with it the risk of European conflict. Faced with this situation, as well as his own serious doubts about involving France in the Spanish war, Blum proposed an international agreement of nonintervention in Spain. By the end of August the major powers had signed such an agreement, although two of the signatories, Germany and Italy, consistently violated the agreement by aiding the Spanish generals.

Blum's refusal to come to the aid of Spanish democracy has been severely criticized by many historians, who have argued that defeat of the Spanish insurgents would have stiffened resistance to Hitler and perhaps prevented the Second World War. The point is very debatable, given Hitler's goals. But Blum's decision can be understood only against the background of his aspirations, political position, and France's position in Europe. Blum himself publicly equated nonintervention in Spain with the cause of peace: in June 1937, he declared "for almost a year, in the midst of one of the most dangerous crises that Europe has ever known, we have preserved peace." Cares other than the preservation of peace were certainly involved. Initially Blum accepted nonintervention in Spain for want of an alternative: stymied by domestic political pressures—opposition of Radicals and Socialists like Paul Faure to any involvement and the threats from the Right—and balked in his efforts to win British support for Madrid, Blum capitulated to reality.

He also became convinced that the danger of European war did exist, and he sought to dispel the threat by appealing for international cooperation and to the "conscience" of the dictators in the hope that nonintervention could be fashioned into a reliable instrument and represent the first step toward the pacification of Europe. Even when this hope was shown to be an illusion, Blum insisted publicly that nonintervention was necessary for peace. His sense of isolation, his fear of war, his inflexible faith in the aspirations of his foreign policy, and his conception of the Popular Front as the conciliator of the nation and reviver of democracy, taken together, were an insurmountable barrier to any reconsideration of nonintervention. Blum believed passionately that France's best interests required internal stability, social reform, and defense of the Republic, and the achievement of a pacified Europe. The Spanish conflict threatened to wreck this vision: at home, he had indications that its impact could provoke civil strife at worst and disintegration of the Popular Front at best if France did not stand aside; internationally, the Spanish Civil War threatened the peace of Europe. Given the situation and Blum's beliefs, his commitment to nonintervention was inevitable: if it was the most satisfactory solution to an awkward political dilemma, it was also fully consistent with his pacifism and his hopes for the France of the Popular Front. In short, Blum gambled that nonintervention would save the Spanish Republic from its assailants, the Popular Front, and peace, and would permit him to pursue his national and international policies. Whether his fears and policies were unrealistic is another matter. Blum gambled and failed, yet the gamble seemed to be preferable to the certainty of immediate failure.

The Blum government also devoted good intentions, but modest attention, to the problems of empire. France's far-flung empire, ranging from Indo-China to North and Black Africa to the Caribbean, including protectorates such as Tunisia and Morocco, and "mandates" such as Syria and the Lebanon from the League of Nations, had been acquired, in large measure, during the earlier years of the Third Republic. The interwar years were a new phase in the development of the empire: the period of acquisition completed, the problem was essentially what to do with the acquisitions. On the surface, with the exception of occasional eruptions in Indo-China, Syria, and North Africa, the empire seemed calm and loyal, even unexciting. In many of these territories, however, developments were taking place that foreshadowed those after the Second World War, which led to the independence of virtually all parts of the empire. During the interwar years the beginnings of the dynamism and drive for independence can be detected, and had the Blum government been able to act on its good intentions, especially with regard to Algeria, perhaps much of the turmoil and strife of the post-1945 era might have been avoided, or at least attenuated.

Unlike Great Britain, whose colonial possessions were regarded as candidates for independence and self-support sometime in the future, the ultimate aim of the French empire was to create a union of "100 million Frenchmen," free and equal, regardless of their place of origin. The British were keenly concerned with the economic development of their possessions, adapted their administration to local habits and traditions, and made little effort to assimilate the natives into their culture. French aims were quite different, and on paper were large and generous: the administrative system and the public services of the mother country were transported, root and branch, to the colonial areas; French culture was imported and given to the native elites, especially via the school system; and everyone agreed that the native population would receive full rights. The real problem was the timetable and manner of receiving these rights, and the organizations of native elites—like the Destour in Tunisia, composed of bourgeois leaders and led in the 1930s by Habib Bourguiba—began to question whether the day of equality would ever arrive, either by independence, as in the case of Tunisia, or by assimilation, as in the case of Algeria. Serious troubles erupted in Indo-China in 1930 and Syria in 1925, but were repressed, and during the 1930s most attention was directed toward North Africa—Tunisia, Morocco, and Algeria, the last named being considered an integral part of France.

In 1936 Habib Bourguiba sought from Blum a commitment to the independence of Tunisia, but was rebuffed; Blum simply could not commit his government to the principle of independence. In 1938 Bourguiba was imprisoned as a result of an abortive uprising in Tunis, which effectively postponed the Tunisian issue until well after the liberation of France in 1944. Morocco in the 1920s had been the virtual fief of Marshal Lyautey, the Governor-General, whose curious blend of modernity and reaction helped to push the protectorate into the twentieth century while preserving her ancient ruling elites by bolstering the feudal powers of the sultan. After the defeat of the insurgent movement led by Abd el Krim, which had spread from Spanish Morocco to the gates of Fez, a young nationalist movement began to emerge in Morocco in the 1930s, the genesis of the movement toward independence finally won in the 1950s. It was Algeria, however, which received most attention from the Blum government and where the chance for the realization of the ideals of empire was best; France may have fumbled a great opportunity in Algeria in the 1930s. In 1934 a movement composed of Algerian elites, desiring neither independence nor assimilation, began to talk of integration, the entrance of Algerians into their full rights as Frenchmen whille preserving their own culture and community. The Blum-Viollette Bill, which never received a full hearing before Parliament, would have granted full citizenship to 20,000–25,000 Algerians without requiring them to abandon their own traditions and obligations to Islamic

Law. The proposal won the approval of Ferhat Abbas, the leader of the Algerian movement, but it met with stern disapproval from the Europeans in Algeria, who took the first step toward their own ruin, which came with Algerian independence in 1962. Had serious integration of the native elites with the French community begun in the 1930s, Algeria might well still be an integral part of France.

THE ILLUSION OF POWER

By the early fall of 1936 it was apparent that the Popular Front program was no longer attuned to reality and the Popular Front partners were becoming entangled in a web of mutual suspicion. Created out of opposition to fascism and need for social reform, the program provided no blueprint to revive a sagging economy and no formula for dealing with the intrusion of foreign affairs as an ideological issue in politics. Although the Blum government was able to survive the impact of the Spanish crisis at the cost of public outrage from the Communists and suspicion of the Communists' intentions by many Socialists and Radicals, both government and spirit of the Popular Front were to suffer a painfully slow death. Buffeted by a complex of problems (the plight of the franc; the absence, despite shifts in government policy, of economic revival; and a renewal of social discontent), hampered by the remarkable convalescence of the conservative forces (revealed by the blustery intransigence of the *patronat*, the unyielding hostility of financial circles, and the belligerent affinity for the rebellion of the Spanish generals in the right-wing press), and undermined by the increasing fragility of its political base, the Blum government stumbled for nine more months along a downward path into immobility and ultimately to abdication.

Compelled to devalue the franc by a sudden acceleration of the outflow of gold in September and a steady rise in prices, which intensified the disparity between French and world prices, the government also signaled a change in its economic policy. Devaluation promised a good deal: by making French prices competitive on the world market, it would aid the export and tourist industries; abandonment of the gold bullion standard relieved the Bank of France of its obligation to redeem its notes in gold and revalorization added seventeen billion francs to the value of the Bank's dwindling gold reserves, ten billion of which were assigned to a newly created Exchange Stabilization Fund, designed to prevent fluctuations in the currency. But speculators, in the absence of exchange control—opposed by the Radicals— were free to obtain other currencies redeemable in gold, and since the franc was still defined as a gold currency, the Treasury was vulnerable to a renewed hemorrhage without warning. The devaluation marked as well an end to faith in the purchasing power theory: the government subsequently staked its hopes for economic improvement on the goodwill of the holders of liquid capital. Blum's new policy sought massive investment in French business by holders of capital-in-exile in the belief that confidence could be attained by opportunities afforded by the devaluation and by government refusal to impose restraints upon exchange control. New investment, it was assumed, would stimulate the economy as a whole.

These expectations proved illusory: the benefits of the devaluation were few and temporary, and the government's wager on the benevolence and patriotism of the financial community was decidedly in error. A continuing rise in prices undercut a moderate improvement in business conditions, and in January 1937, speculative pressure against the franc exhausted the coffers of the Exchange Stabilization Fund. New investments were not forthcoming. Thus in February the government opted for further concessions to liberal capitalism, this time in the hope of securing at least the neutrality of the financial groups. The "pause," announced by Blum on February 14, promised that the government would do nothing to alarm its detractors: abandoned were new social welfare schemes and public works projects for which funds had already been allocated, and three so-called experts highly esteemed in financial circles were appointed to oversee the workings of the Exchange Stabilization Fund. The "pause" in substance was a promise to do nothing at all: it was a desperate bid to halt speculation against the franc. Henceforth, the government survived only on the sufferance of its most inveterate opponents.

Blum was also ill-treated by his political allies: the victim of sniping from both flanks of the Popular Front in 1936, he received better treatment in the spring of 1937 only because neither Communists nor Radicals could propose a viable alternative to his remaining in power. The Communists, angered by their inability to force a change in French policy toward Spain and by the devaluation, which struck hardest at their working-class clientele, mounted a sharp assault upon the Premier in the fall of 1936 featuring a charge by Thorez that Blum was capitulating to Hitler. But the Communists could do little else but launch verbal tirades and annoying strikes: they were the prisoners of their own limited aspirations. Their failure to vote against the government in the Chamber debate over foreign policy in December demonstrated that, whatever their talent for invective and nuisance, they could not risk a rupture of the Popular Front. The Radicals, visibly worried by Communist bellicosity over Spain (exemplified by the slogan "guns and planes for Spain" featured at Communist rallies), alarmed by what appeared to be Communist-inspired labor difficulties, and increasingly susceptible to the strident anti-Popular Front warnings of their right-wing, seemed to be preparing their exit from the Popular Front. When the government settled into immobility in early 1937, however, the Radicals had neither reason nor occasion to topple it. Yet Radicals had clearly begun their journey away from the Popular Front, which was to culminate in 1938 with their outright alliance with the conservative camp. The Radicals, in short, were running true to form.

There is little useful purpose in subjecting all of Blum's problems to careful scrutiny, but several deserve mention: the leaders of the CGT, mesmerized by the redemptive myth of the forty-hour week, pushed for immediate and complete implementation of the forty-hour law and other measures dear to their hearts; the *patronat*, reorganized by tough-minded businessmen and emboldened by the cracks in the Popular Front, brusquely rejected renewal of the bargaining contracts that had followed the Matignon Agreements; work on the International Exposition of 1937 in Paris, intended to symbolize France's revival, fell far behind schedule because of workers' slowdowns; and the bloody riot at Clichy on March 16, whether due to exasperation of the working class with the lassitude of the government, or simple blunder on the part of the authorities, dealt a sharp blow to Blum's withering self-confidence. Blum's vision of the Popular Front, which presupposed a minimum of national cohesiveness for its success, ran afoul of the refusal of each sector of French society to look beyond its own narrow interests.

These problems, however, were subsidiary to the interlocking problems of economic stagnation and financial instability. The government's patient efforts at conciliating its antagonists failed to correct the illness of the franc, and the lack of any apparent economic revival increased budgetary disequilibrium. In May a new speculative assault upon the franc began, and the more that the government vowed that another devaluation was out of the question the more certain did devaluation appear to speculators. The crisis became a panic in June, and the money market refused to absorb the short-term government bonds to replace those falling due. The financial watchdogs appointed to the Exchange Stabilization Fund attempted to extort from Blum a pledge to make rigid economies in expenditure and to refuse to consider control over monetary exchanges. Blum had to reject their demands: acceptance would have implied a full-fledged return to conservative economics, involving not merely the renunciation of further social measures but the repeal of some already enacted. The resignation of the financial watchdogs appeared to be the first act in a showdown between Blum and his assailants.

However, the showdown was not forthcoming: Blum chose to withdraw with honor, and honor required that the parliamentary game be played out. The Premier asked the Parliament for decree powers to deal with the financial panic, but made no effort to reassure the financial community as he had done in October and February. Although Auriol was fuzzy in his explanations of what would be done with these powers should they be granted, it was an open secret that the government would institute a rigid control over exchanges. The Chamber of Deputies voted its approval of the proposal, as most of the Radicals maintained the fiction of support for the Popular Front, serenely confident that their elderly colleagues in the Senate would do their work for them. The Senate obliged with a massive rejection of the legislation, and rather than appealing to the Chamber for a vote of confidence—which might have provoked a constitutional crisis had the government won the vote—Blum submitted his resignation to a relieved President of the Republic. The great experiment was over.

Why did Blum succumb to the will of the Senate and the financial community without making any use of the legal and extralegal weapons at his disposal? Several of his colleagues urged him to demand a vote of confidence from the Chamber, thereby pitting the Chamber against the Senate, and then to ask for a dissolution of the Chamber to be followed by a new election. This election would be fought on an emotional issue, the right of the Senate to overthrow a government resting on a majority elected by universal suffrage. A Popular Front electoral victory would enable the government to smash the obstructionist Senate and to carry out structural reforms of the economy, including selected nationalizations. Some Socialists, like Pivert and Zyromski, demanded that Blum employ the threat of popular force against the Senate by an appeal to the workers of Paris. Blum calmly refused to follow either course, and withdrew. Was this simply a confession of fatigue and failure?

Blum was mindful of harsh political realities: neither Communists nor Radicals were prepared to enter the lists to keep the government in office. The Communists had no desire to see France plunge into turmoil: a weak France was of no use to the Soviet Union, and the Communists still believed that their purpose stood better chance of achievement under a Radical government. The Radical ministers asked Blum not to call for a vote of confidence, clearly implying that a majority of their party might not support the government.

More important than purely political factors was Blum's fidelity to his socialist beliefs and to his conception of the Popular Front, as well as to his assessment of the international situation, which he had seen worsen during his term of power. At the Socialist Congress, held after his resignation, Blum declared that had popular force been unleashed, the aim would have been revolution; there was no middle way. But the very nature of Blum's socialism compelled him to oppose such a venture: he believed that the workers could not move to take power until they were completely prepared to carry out a social revolution. Surely he had no indication that that moment had in fact arrived, and on numerous occasions he had called for patience and adherence to "legality." Blum's conception of the Popular Front represented an even more serious barrier to the employment of mass pressure; likewise it militated against the deliberate provocation of a constitutional crisis. Blum recalled that the Popular Front was not responsible to the proletariat alone, but to the entire nation; its aim was national revival. Illegal proletarian action could, in Blum's view, provoke a social crisis that would divide the nation yet further. Finally, Blum's assessment of the international situation affected his decision: frustrated by his fruitless effort to ameliorate relations with Nazi Germany and worried by massive Italian and German involvement in Spain, Blum declared that he "did not have the right" to provoke an internal crisis in time of peril for France.

In fact Blum knew that he was defeated, and that his hopes for the Popular Front were doomed to partial fulfillment. Long before, he had assured his countrymen that he would not play the role of Kerensky; and he was not going to take the doubtful road of revolution himself. The task of the Popular Front was finished: it had won great social gains for the masses, and hopefully the Radicals would be the guardians of the achievement; if it had failed to pacify Europe, it had, for a brief moment, symbolized the aspiration for goodwill among all nations. Blum simply had no reason to hang on to power, which itself was now only an illusion. Unless the liberal capitalist institutions were to be restructured considerably—and the time was not, to Blum, one for revolutionary alterations—enactment of further reforms was impossible. Blum was already concerned that a new political alignment, broader than the Popular Front, could emerge and give the nation the unity and determination that the Popular Front could no longer hope to provide.

Blum's dilemma was that of the Popular Front itself: when power was shown to be an illusion, there could be no middle way. There were only two ways out, one by a revolutionary attempt at political as well as social change, the other by strategic withdrawal. Perhaps it was impossible to wed government-sponsored social innovation with the economic conservatism of the business and industrial structure on the one hand and the desire to transform the social system with the maintenance of the parliamentary regime on the other. Stalemate and deepening division of the nation were contrary to the creed and spirit of the Popular Front, and the limbo in which the Popular Front lived after January 1937 simply could not last. As one historian-participant of the Popular Front observed, it was struck dead from early 1937, but was condemned to endure a living death until 1938.[4] Yet the Popular Front was not a failure. Generated by fear for the future of democracy, moved by generous enthusiasm and popular participation, it may have given birth to expectations that were impossible to attain in its time. Although for some it was only a great adventure, it did accomplish much that it set out to do. Its original aim had been to guarantee and protect the Republic, to provide a measure of social amelioration, and to revive faith in democracy; it had not been created to carry out drastic renovation. The Republic would continue, at least until 1940, and democracy would be reborn in 1944; social gains would be emasculated in 1938, but were revived after 1944 by

[4] Georges Lefranc, *Histoire du Front Populaire* (Paris, 1965).

many of the same men who had made the Popular Front; and, through Léon Blum, France sought to show Europeans the futility of war.

Finally, in a Europe darkened by totalitarianism, France did attempt to reassert the vitality of democracy; the Popular Front was eminently the product of the French democratic tradition and was an effort by part of the French nation to realize the greatness of its heritage. Léon Blum was right when he told his accusers at a trial staged by the Vichy regime that "in a troubled era, we personified and revived the authentic tradition of this country, which is the Republican and democratic tradition. We were not some hideous monster because we were a people's government; we were in the tradition of this country since the French Revolution. We did not interrupt the chain, nor did we break it, but we renewed and reasserted it. Freedom and justice have not made this country a disarmed prey."

6 / The Last Days
of the Republic,
1938-1940

Parliament must take the blame upon its shoulders for the faults of all. This crucifixion is necessary in order that the country shall not lapse into violence and anarchy. The past was filled with illusion and, if the horizons of the world seemed to conform to them, it was but a mirage. We have believed in individual liberty and the independence of man. These were but anticipations of a future which was not within our reach. We must have a new faith built upon new values.

CHARLES SPINASSE, SOCIALIST LEADER, AT VICHY, 1940

We must destroy all that is. Then, the destruction completed, we must create something that will be entirely different from what has been, from what is. We have been living through years in which it seemed of no importance to say of a man that he was a thief, a swindler, a pimp, or even a murderer. But if one said of him "he is a fascist," then one said the worst thing that was possible! Today we are paying for the fetishism which has chained us to democracy and delivered us to the worst excesses of capitalism, while all about us Europe was creating a new world without us, a world founded upon new principles.

PIERRE LAVAL AT VICHY, 1940

The ease with which Blum was removed from office and the slide of the Radicals toward concentration with parties to their right during the second half of 1937 and the early months of

113

1938 demonstrated that what had been diagnosed as the fatal illness of the Republican synthesis was in fact only a precarious convalescence. The Popular Front lived in name only under two governments led by the Radical conciliator Camille Chautemps, a short-lived government led by Blum in the spring of 1938, and the subsequent government headed by Daladier. Social reform and urgent defense of the Republic were no longer on the political calendar: hanging on to power and abandoning it when it was no longer attractive on the eve of Hitler's takeover of Austria were Chautemps' concerns; Blum unsuccessfully sought to weld together a national union in response to the alarming threat of German aggression, and once again abdicated with honor over the tired issue of finance; and Daladier formally buried the Popular Front and carried out a frankly conservative economic policy, winning the applause and support of many of those who had reviled him in 1934.

Times indeed had changed: the primary concerns now were those of foreign policy in a Europe edging closer to armed conflict. Instead of enthusiasm and adventure, Frenchmen watched a diplomacy that was less than heroic culminate in war, a war that no one wanted but most were resigned to accept. Yet the legacy of fear and hate from the immediate past was not to be effaced, and it spilled over into diplomacy and the conduct of war. At the time of tragic defeat in 1940, the partisans of ideological revenge against the Republic and the Popular Front joined hands with those who were united only in despair for their country to write the last chapter in the history of the Third Republic.

THE ARMY OF THE NATION

Much has been written, and continues to be written, about the French Army as it marched toward catastrophe in 1940. General André Beaufre summarized the consensus of opinion when he wrote that "the French Army was nothing more than a vast, inefficient tool, incapable of quick reaction or adaption," with a General Staff deprived of all constructive thought, and without a will to victory in 1939–1940. Despite the ambitions of French diplomacy, which provided protection to Poland, Czechoslovakia, Rumania, and Yugoslavia, the French Army was a tool for defense only. For example, when Hitler reoccupied the Rhineland in 1936, the Chief of the General Staff, General Gamelin, protested that only a general mobilization could provide sufficient force to push the Germans back. In numbers and equipment—much bolstered by the Popular Front government of Léon Blum—France's military was generally thought to be the equal of Germany's, and very few suspected that it was not. The allegedly impregnable Maginot Line, coupled with the defensive strategy developed from the experience of the First World War, gave French soldiers a sense of complete security: they never for a moment thought that they would lose a war, although the chief of the air force had some bad moments when he witnessed a display by the *Luftwaffe*. Admitting that France could not come directly to the assistance of her eastern friends, the General Staff assumed that a stalwart defense, plus some diversionary thrusts across the German frontier, a blockade of Germany, and time, would assure ultimate victory. The strategy was not glamorous, but it seemed solid. By avoiding the offensive strategy of the First World War and thus limiting casualties and drain on French resources, the General Staff was confident of success. Confidence so quickly shattered in 1940 was a severe psychological blow, effectively prohibiting serious and prolonged resistance to the enemy. The French military was, in substance, too confident for its own good; the possibility that its defenses could be breached was never seriously considered, and contingency plans were barely prepared.

Of itself, the strategy was basically sound, but it was undermined by the officer corps' remarkable insularity from new ideas, the most attractive being Colonel de Gaulle's proposal for the creation of highly mobile armored units to compensate for the fact that French tanks were too slow and too heavy. Not only did the military fail to complete one of the pillars of its own strategy by the extension of the Maginot Line across the Belgian frontier, but it also failed to appreciate the technological strides that the potential enemy was making. The most grievous error committed by the military planners was their failure to comprehend that a new means of defense against a new kind of warfare might be necessary. Imprisoned by their memories of the First World War, the generals did not understand the need for swifter tanks and the means to shift forces from one point to another rapidly, and despite numerous warnings, they ignored the dramatic changes in the German Army—even after Germany's lightening invasion of Poland in 1939, characterized by the success of swift, highly mobile tank and armored units.

Poor planning, and poor execution of that planning, were primary causes of the military disaster of 1940. Yet why should this have been so? Why should an army, apparently victorious in the greatest war in human history, have been unable to make accommodations with reality and to demonstrate a capacity for innovation? Much of the answer lies in the nature and concerns of the officer corps and in the character of the military leaders themselves. It is not enough to point out that the top generals, Weygand and Gamelin, were advanced in years, that Marshal Pétain, very advanced in years, was extremely influential, and that the officer corps confidently expected to fight the First World War all over again. Age, experience, and a reluctance to be imaginative do not necessarily spell disaster.

It cannot be overemphasized that the officer corps was a class apart from the nation, and a class with self-assigned and ambitious responsibilities; the military was one of several compartments of French society, a compartment with its own hierarchy, rules, and principles. The top of the hierarchy was elderly and very conservative, and not without memory of the humiliation of the Army by the politicians during the Dreyfus affair at the turn of the century. Their political sentiments were only sentiments and not an ideology, but most were very conservative and some retained a hankering after monarchy, if only as an ideal. Their essential concern was the maintenance of the rights and privileges of the Army itself, in order to keep it immune to corroding outside influences, especially from the politicians.

General Maxime Weygand, Chief of the General Staff from

1930 to 1935, embodied the virtues and vices of the French officer to a disastrous perfection.[1] His indifference to the Republic helped to maintain his tenuous allegiance to it, and he guarded the prerogatives of his fellows with scrupulous care, slashing out against the proponents of disarmament and engaging in running conflict with politicians like Daladier. Weygand felt himself humiliated by parliamentary questions about the conduct of his office, as if the military should be exempt from criticism and investigation by the regime to which loyalty was ostensibly due. Although Weygand refused association with the men of the sixth of February, he certainly had sympathy with their aims, and his authoritarian reflexes grew stronger with age. It was an easy step for Weygand and many of his comrades, especially in a period of political and social turmoil, to identify the Army with the nation, to see the Army as the guardian of the nation, and to believe that the Army's own peculiar morality should be emulated by the nation, if necessary by force. Increasingly grave disaffection with the regime was hidden during General Gamelin's tenure as Chief of the General Staff, beginning in 1935, but this disaffection was to emerge full-blown in 1940, and General Weygand was to be one of its coordinators. Thus the Army was not only obsessed with its lifeless strategy and its self-serving concept of itself and its role within the nation, but it began to regard the Republic as unworthy of the nation.

THE DIPLOMACY OF WEAKNESS

The record of French diplomacy in 1938 and 1939 is as lamentable as it is familiar. The reader will recall the several tacks taken by French diplomacy since Versailles, all of which had proved unrewarding: the harshness of Poincaré, the flexibility of Briand, the firmness of Tardieu, the deviousness of Laval, and the idealism of Blum were succeeded by the weak-

---

[1] See Philip C. F. Bankwitz, *Maxime Weygand and Civil-Military Relations in Modern France* (Cambridge, Mass., 1967).

ness of Daladier and his Foreign Minister, Georges Bonnet. All of the previous policies had rested, in differing degree, upon French initiative and had presupposed that France could take independent action, although Blum had undergone a sobering experience in his relations with London. The diplomacy of Daladier and Bonnet was cast in a British mold, even though it had French trappings and many French leaders cultivated the illusion that France's fate was her own to decide. French initiative was closely circumscribed by the government's conviction that alliance with Britain was a *sine qua non* of French security, and indeed it was; yet Daladier and Bonnet were all too willing followers in Neville Chamberlain's search for appeasement. French diplomacy reacted—to Berlin and London—and only rarely, and briefly, sought to control events; bluster was invariably followed by retreat.

Domestic pressures also contributed to the government's behavior, although the question of resistance or nonresistance to Nazi demands cut across all political and social boundaries. It is not improbable that a majority of Frenchmen were opposed to dying for Czechoslovakia in 1938, but that they were resigned to do so for Poland in 1939. It would be tempting to argue that the split over the wisdom of appeasement was along Left/Right lines, with the Left, acting out of its commitment to combat fascism, for resistance to Germany, and the Right, acting out of fear of destroying Nazi Germany as a bulwark against communism, in favor of appeasement. In several individual cases, this formula does in fact apply, but it is inapplicable as a general rule. There were almost as many appeasers on the Left as on the Right, and almost as many resisters on the Right as on the Left. Such division did not facilitate the government's task, even if it had had the will to formulate a firm and unyielding diplomacy, which it did not have.

At the time of the *Anschluss* between Germany and Austria in March 1938, France was without a government because of the sudden resignation of Camille Chautemps a few days before. Partly as a result, France did nothing to counter the German move, and some Paris newspapers rationalized that if Austrians wanted to be incorporated into the *Reich*, then what harm was done? After all, it was only an affair among Germans. A short-lived government headed by Léon Blum, who, much alarmed by Hitler's action, began to shift quickly toward a policy of firmness toward Germany, reaffirmed the totality of France's commitments to Czechoslovakia.

Daladier and Bonnet, in office in late April, shared Blum's concern that Czechoslovakia might be the next victim of the Nazi appetite, but they responded to the threat in differing ways. Daladier and Bonnet were not well suited to work in tandem, although both excelled in the unhappy art of making enemies. Daladier oscillated between extremes, adopting one day what he had argued vehemently against the day before; no more vocal opponent of appeasement changed his mind so profoundly or so often. Bonnet, a shadowy figure among conservative Radicals, had been a minister in several governments, and was especially appreciated by the financial community. Despite his remarkable talent for defending his own actions, it seems clear that Bonnet decidedly figured among the appeasers and was firm only in his determination that France should be spared another war. The result of Daladier-Bonnet direction in foreign affairs was acquiescence to the British lead, especially in the summer of 1938 when Chamberlain vigorously sought to scuttle Czechoslovakia before her existence precipitated a general war. Although it was France which had an alliance with the Czechs, it was Chamberlain who went to meet the Führer in the now-famous sessions at Berchtesgaden and Godesberg in an attempt to make Hitler reasonable at the expense of the integrity of Czechoslovakia, and the French were only consulted about what was transpiring. In late September, when it appeared that a general war was all but inevitable, Daladier readied mobilization of France's armed forces and spoke gravely about the need for France to honor her word to Czechoslovakia. Yet Daladier sped off to Munich and agreed to the amputation of Czech territory, winning only Britain's guarantee of the rump

Czechoslovak state.[2] Unlike Chamberlain, Daladier believed that Munich had been a heavy defeat, and viewing the crowds swarming about the airport upon his arrival in Paris, Daladier thought that they had come to lynch him. Much to his surprise he discovered a joyous throng, led by Georges Bonnet, congratulating him for work well done; "the fools," Daladier was heard to mutter.

In retrospect, the only thing France really did lose at Munich was her honor; what she surrendered had already been lost. France acknowledged that her commitments to her eastern allies were basically paper commitments, something that her military strategy had determined long before, and for the first time military policy and diplomacy were in harmony. France did not surrender her own security, since her leaders, civil and military, were certain that France could defend her own frontiers. Czechoslovakia, like Poland, was more of a burden than a help to France. France simply confessed that she was no longer the policeman of Europe, although it must be admitted that the confession was unlikely to deter Hitler from making further territorial demands and may have convinced him that he could make not one, but many Munichs.

Most of France expressed profound relief at the news of the conclusion of the Munich accord. Even Léon Blum, who had begun to urge a policy of firmness on the government, announced that "there is not a man or a woman in France who can refuse to Mr. Chamberlain and Edouard Daladier his just tribute of gratitude," and his comrade Paul Faure described Munich as "the victory of Peace." Pierre-Etienne Flandin sent a congratulatory telegram to Hitler. The right-wing journal *Je Suis Partout* observed that it was better to live for France than to die for the Czechs, Jews, or "Red Spain," and launched a campaign to dissolve the Communist Party, described as "a

[2] For details of the events preceding Munich and the conference itself, see A. J. P. Taylor, *The Origins of the Second World War* (London, 1961), J. W. Wheeler-Bennett, *Munich: Prologue to Tragedy* (London, 1948), Keith Eubank, *Munich* (Norman, Okla., 1963), and Alexander Werth, *France and Munich* (New York, 1939).

foreign army on French soil" after it was the only party to vote against approval of Daladier's conduct of foreign affairs. Approval was temporarily almost unanimous, especially among the peasantry, whose spokesmen expressed their joy that peace had been preserved.

Second thoughts, however, were not long in emerging. Once tension had eased, many political leaders wondered aloud whether the Munich formula would set a pattern for the future and whether France could afford the price. Intense debate over the future direction of French diplomacy took place within every political group: Socialists ruined their party as an effective political force by their inability to compromise, with half of the SFIO lining up behind Blum's insistence that France forge firm alliances with the determination to fight German aggression, and the other half behind Paul Faure, who feared Stalin more than Hitler, insisting that peace be preserved almost at any price. On the Right, Henri de Kérillis and André Tardieu denounced Munich as a defeat for France, while the *Action Française* and Jacques Doriot considered appeasement a viable and necessary policy (perhaps to stave off the revolution they still feared at home); Doriot's posture alienated many of his followers who were forced to choose between the humiliation of their nation and agreement with those whom they had denounced as warmongers. Even Colonel de la Rocque declared that France should be ready to go to war to defend her honor and her commitments. Most of the right-wing apologists for appeasement defended their position on the ground that France's vital interests were not at stake, that the German demands were just, and that Moscow was attempting to provoke a general European war. The old nationalist conservative, Louis Marin, along with the Radical journalist Pierre Dominique, urged that France revive her ties with Italy in the expectation that a Franco-Italian alignment would deter German ambitions and pave the way for a general European rapprochement. Many solutions, then, were offered, but only one was pursued—the choice was to follow the British lead.

Edouard Daladier took advantage of the dislocation of the

political groups over foreign policy to complete a reorientation of domestic policy by burying the ossified corpse of the Popular Front. The government was granted full powers to legislate by decree in financial and economic matters against the opposition of the Communists and the abstention of the Socialists, thus formally breaking the Popular Front parliamentary alliance. A new majority—331 against 281—was created, and the Radicals had once again come full circle. Daladier openly attacked the Communists as bellicose and demagogic, provoking a savage retort from the leaders of the CGT.

The new Minister of Finance, Paul Reynaud, published a series of decree-laws limiting the application of the forty-hour work week, the practice of two consecutive days off, and vacations that closed down factories for two weeks. Reynaud also increased taxes and asked for heavy voluntary sacrifices so that production, and especially armaments production, could be accelerated, but he imposed no limitations on speculators, refusing to impose control over monetary exchange; in other words, it was the workers who were to make the sacrifices. The CGT protested against the "decree-laws of misery," several strikes broke out, and a sit-down strike was smashed by armed force. The CGT then decided upon a general strike for November 30, which was unsuccessful, as public services functioned normally. Daladier's victory was complete, and he took his revenge, suspending more than a thousand functionaries, dismissing others, and bringing criminal charges against others; even Léon Jouhaux was discharged from his nominal post on the Board of Governors of the Bank of France. If he could not be firm in foreign policy, Daladier could be ruthless in domestic matters, and his public demolition of the Popular Front and humiliation of labor brought its reward in a sharp upswing in the amount of capital flowing into the country. At the very least, France seemed to have found a means to bring about her economic revival.

After signing what he regarded as a splendid "friendship treaty" with Germany in December, Bonnet began to make overtures to Rome early in 1939, once again chasing the illusion of Mussolini's reliability as a stabilizing force for peace. But Daladier now seemed to be made of sterner stuff, making a well-publicized tour of France's North African possessions indicating France's complete rejection of Italian colonial demands at her expense, and he continued to step up the pace of rearmament by increasing the working week in armaments factories. When Hitler seized control of the rest of Czechoslovakia in March 1939, in violation of the Munich agreement, the French government was quick to prod London to make its position clear with regard to any future German aggression. Britain's guarantee to Poland strengthened Daladier's hand and his will, and the clear shift by many of those who had been in favor of appeasement toward firmness shored up his resolve.

Socialists still remained evenly divided, with their pacifist wing apparently on the ascendancy, but many on the Right reverted to their old anti-German position, although many conservatives still balked at alliance with the Soviet Union. The reasons for the shift on the Right are obvious: Hitler had committed an outrageous act, the Daladier government could not be accused of wanting ideological war, Daladier had cut loose his ties with his friends on the Left, and the government's orthodox economic policies had sparked a modest economic resurgence. In the summer of 1939 many conservative newspapers, including the passionately anti-Communist Catholic press, supported the Anglo-French bid for alliance with the Soviets, which of course was stillborn thanks to much footdragging by Paris and London and the conclusion of the Nazi-Soviet Pact on August 22. In the final crisis before the outbreak of the war, France again took second place to Britain in the frantic negotiations designed to avert war over Poland, and there are indications that had another Munich been arranged, the French government would have succumbed to the temptation to purchase peace at the price of honor.[3] In any event, when Hitler invaded Poland and ignored France's admonition to withdraw, France had no alternative but to fulfil her commitments to her ally. Whatever hesitations, divisions, and

[3] See A. J. P. Taylor, *The Origins of the Second World War* (London, 1961), chap. XI.

reluctance it may have had, the French nation declared war on Germany on September 3, 1939.

DISASTER

Unlike 1914, when enthusiasm for war was contagious and crowds surged through the streets crying "To Berlin!", Frenchmen entered war in 1939 with somber resignation; no one witnessed any display of enthusiasm. From the outset, there were many who opposed the war and campaigned actively against it, whether in the press, the corridors of the Chamber, or in the factories. The Communists, executing another about-face, thanks to the Nazi-Soviet Pact and to Soviet neutrality, were transformed from antifascist crusaders into bleating pacifists who denounced the "imperialist war" and the senseless slaughter awaiting French soldiers. The attitude of most Communists should have ruined them forever, but Daladier's energetic and ruthless suppression of the Communist Party, thereby preventing the party's press from publicizing its almost treasonous message, worked to its ultimate advantage. Communist deputies were arrested, Communist union offcials were incarcerated, and the party dissolved; it looked as if the workers' representatives were being singled out for repression, and the government's vigorous crackdown on labor, destroying what was left of the Popular Front reforms, suspending the rights of collective bargaining and arbitration, and providing for overtime at reduced wages, seemed to indicate that the workers were being excluded from the nation once again. Thus the Communists escaped the condemnation of the workers, and the fate that they deserved. When the Soviet Union was attacked by Hitler in 1941, French Communists flocked into the Resistance, essentially effacing their dismal record of 1939–1940.

Suppression of the Communists seemed especially unfair when others whose views on the war were not too dissimilar were permitted to express themselves openly: a so-called peace party began to form around Paul Faure, the ex-Socialist Marcel Déat, Flandin, Laval, Doriot, and Bonnet (whose removal as

Foreign Minister in September was a positive sign that the government was indeed determined to do something), and, supported by parts of the right-wing press and parts of the Socialist press, they agitated for an end to the war once Poland had been defeated. Some elements on the Right accused the Popular Front of being responsible for a war for which France was not prepared—a charge that the Vichy regime was later to make—and were not reluctant to express frankly defeatist sentiments; likewise Socialist followers of Paul Faure upbraided many of their colleagues for abandoning traditional Socialist pacifism. Daladier made no move against these defeatists: to crush the Communists was popular with his parliamentary majority, but much of his support rested upon parties and groups that contained sizable numbers of defeatists. Even after war had begun, it appears that political considerations took precedence over the need to rally the nation against the enemy.

One reason that France momentarily could afford the luxury of diversity over the war was the fact that the war seemed unreal. Until May 1940, Hitler undertook no action against France, although he did march into Norway in April; aside from a few hasty expeditions into German territory, France made no serious moves against Germany. These months were labeled the period of the "phony war," and they may have taken their toll in lassitude and loss of zeal to fight on the French side. In any event, France did not employ the respite to prepare furiously for the coming struggle. The production of heavy armaments was limited by budgetary considerations, and the changeover to new and swifter types of aircraft was hardly a crash program to achieve parity with the enemy. France was settling down for a long siege or for a diplomatic breakthrough, and she may have lost an opportunity to strengthen her armed forces appreciably; yet such strengthening may not have made any difference. Daladier did make a comical effort to persuade the United States to build 10,000 planes for France, pledging a mortgage on France's historical monuments if necessary, but isolationist America turned a deaf ear. Following his usual pattern, Daladier wavered between firmness and anxiety, and even expressed despair bordering on defeatism. Following his refusal to send an expeditionary force to Finland to assist her against Soviet aggression, Daladier was brought down in March by a combination of defeatists, rightists angered by his unwillingness to fight Stalin in Finland, and those anxious for a more vigorous prosecution of war preparations. Daladier was replaced by Paul Reynaud, famous for his conservative economic policy and his consistent stand for firmness against Germany. Reynaud was no Clemenceau: his cabinet was built upon compromise, upon the political need to include proponents of firmness as well as partisans of conciliation as a means to end the war, and he kept Daladier, with whom his realtions had deteriorated, as Defense Minister. Even with such elaborate compromise, Reynaud was approved by the Chamber with a single-vote majority. It did not appear that Reynaud could play the role of Clemenceau even if he had the will and decisiveness to do so; the pity was that there was no other candidate even remotely qualified to play the role.

Belgium had proclaimed her neutrality in 1936, so French troops could not swing into her territory until German troops crossed the Belgian frontiers, as the French confidently expected them to do. When, on May 10, 1940, Hitler invaded Belgium, French troops departed from their defensive positions along the frontier in order to aid Belgium and Holland, similarly invaded. Many observers have seen this move as a tactical blunder, since it isolated French forces in the north, although it was a political necessity to show that France was willing to fight for others. The swiftness of the German assault was devastating: employing highly mobile tanks and dive bombers, the Germans swept through the supposedly impenetrable Ardennes forest, liquidated French resistance in that sector, captured Sedan on the thirteenth and moved on Abbeville, effectively cutting off the French forces in the north, which had fought well against the invader. Poor communications, irregular liaison between land and air forces, and transport bogged down by the flow of refugees severely hampered French operations, and, as the Germans moved north to confront the trapped French and British forces around Dunkerque, the only escape was evacuation by sea, which was executed magnificently.

General Weygand was summoned home from Syria to replace Gamelin, but the situation was virtually beyond hope; Weygand's own deep pessimism about his chances for success was not something expected from a new commander who had been appointed to buoy the dispirited officers and politicians. On June 10 Paris was declared an open city, and the government moved in haste to Bordeaux. On May 18 Reynaud had appointed Marshal Pétain his Vice-Premier in an obvious effort to rally the national will, although the Marshal had little confidence in a favorable outcome. As the French forces fell back and the Nazis occupied Paris, intense debate began within the government whether to continue resistance, and, if so, from where.

Initially interested by the idea of a "Breton redoubt," which was dismissed as impracticable, Reynaud was determined to carry on the struggle from North Africa aided by the vast resources of the French Empire. Preparations were in fact made to evacuate the government to Algiers, and many politicians embarked for North Africa, and the President of the Republic was expecting to depart shortly afterward. Reynaud's plan would involve an armistice in France. To Reynaud's shock, General Weygand absolutely refused to consider a military armistice unless it was negotiated by the government as a total cessation of hostilities; when he was reminded that the Queen of Holland had fled Holland to set up a government-in-exile, Weygand allegedly remarked that this was a matter of royalty, not a "matter of one of our puny Republican governments." Weygand's disobedience to the civil authority was clear-cut: he refused to consider any alternative to an armistice, and the majority of the government, on June 16, voted to ask Germany her conditions for an armistice. Weygand's insubordination may well have been crucial in the government's decision, as he was supported by Marshal Pétain; Weygand's decision was the logical product of his concept of the Army and of the Army's place in the nation. A stronger leader would have arrested Weygand on the spot, but Reynaud chose instead to resign. Pétain was appointed Prime Minister, and on June 22 he secured an armistice that provided for German occupation of three-fifths of France and the reduction of the French Army to 100,000 men. On June 24, France and Italy (whose forces had invaded France on June 10, when it was eminently safe to do so) concluded an armistice. France had lost the war of 1940.

VICHY

"For two days I watched men debasing themselves, becoming corrupt beneath one's eyes, as if they had been plunged into a bath of poison. They were possessed by fear: fear of Doriot's gangs in the streets, fear of Weygand's soldiers at Clermont-Ferrand, fear of the Germans who were at Moulins. It was a human swamp in which one saw beneath one's very eyes the courage and integrity one had known in certain men dissolve, corrode, and disappear." So wrote an anguished Léon Blum of the events at Vichy, to. which the government had repaired, on July 9 and 10, 1940. By a vote of 569 to 80 the National Assembly, composed of the Senate and Chamber meeting jointly in constitutional session, sent the Third Republic to its death and authorized Marshal Pétain to create a new regime, presumably on an authoritarian model.

However tawdry the episode, explanations as to why and how it happened are appallingly simple, no matter how much has been written about it.[4] There were few solid and courageous defenders of democracy at Vichy in 1940 precisely because democracy no longer seemed worth defending; the parliamentarians were persuaded of their own incapacity to rule and of the failure of the Republic. The statements of Charles Spinasse and Pierre Laval, cited at the beginning of this chapter, personified the broken spirit of the moment: democracy had been wrong because it was weak, and weak because it had ignored the dynamism of the "new Europe" being created all around it.

[4] See the Bibliography.

The shock of a defeat of such magnitude and the fear that hung over everyone present helped to create the "human swamp" that Blum described so well. To men who were emotionally and intellectually disarmed, the words of Pierre Laval had the ring of truth: "Do you imagine that we still have time to listen to speeches? You are wrong: speeches are done with. We are not here for you to make speeches nor are we here to listen to them. We have to rebuild France. We must destroy all that is. Then, the destruction accomplished, we must create something that will be entirely different from what has been, from what now exists. There are only two alternatives: either you accept what we demand, and align yourselves with the German and Italian constitutions, or Hitler will impose one upon you."

How striking, yet how symbolic it was that an elderly figure from the past should have embodied French hopes for renewal and that the most devious practitioner of the discredited art of Republican politics should have been the chief executioner of the Republic. Marshal Pétain and Pierre Laval were an implausible team, but they were men suited to the moment. Pétain, the "hero of Verdun," respected as few military figures could have been, was a comforting if not inspiring figure, and his vow to remain in France so that his person could represent a mortgage for the safety of Frenchmen had considerable appeal. Pétain saw that his duty was to ameliorate the conditions of his countrymen in an agonizing moment of their history, to bargain with the Germans wherever possible, and to maintain a regime as independent of the Germans as the situation would permit; this would require a regime with authority, and he was not at all averse to the indefinite suspension of democracy. Laval, who had been in political limbo since the fall of his government in 1936, was determined to create a regime that would have a legitimate place in the "new Europe" of Adolf Hitler. Appointed Vice-Premier on June 23, Laval, working closely with the sinister Adrien Marquet and other persons whose affinity for fascism was well known, set about his work of demolition with zeal. The politicians who had fled to North Africa were denounced as traitors, and the Marshal was persuaded to issue a national appeal for "moral regeneration," clearly implying a realignment of political institutions.

At Vichy, the headquarters of a government which ruled only unoccupied France, two-fifths of the national territory, Laval and his agents employed flattery and threats in their dealings with the parliamentarians. Their arguments struck responsive chords: the defeat was the responsibility of the Republic, which had failed the nation; unity instead of political divisiveness was mandatory, and only by giving full power to the Marshal could such unity be attained; unless France cleaned out her own house, Hitler would do the job; and that Britain would soon surrender, leaving Hitler master of Europe. Together with outright threats and displays of strength, such as Doriot's goon squads on parade, the weight of Laval's arguments made his success almost a foregone conclusion, despite feeble efforts by some politicians to sidetrack him. Laval himself dominated the public sessions, and Republican stalwarts like Blum sat silent as the Republic was vilified; fear, despondency, guilt, and, in Blum's case, humiliation—he knew a majority of the Socialists would vote for full powers to the Marshal—stilled many of the old prominent voices. And, at voting time, only 80 men of 649 stood in defense of the Third Republic.

7 / Conclusion

Those who condemned the Republic were themselves condemned only five years later, but their verdict on the Republic
has not been effaced. Indeed many of those who supported the
Republic in 1940 were among its severest critics: Léon Blum
decried the immobility of the bourgeoisie and its political parties, alleging the failure of the political class to be faithful to its
own ideals, and Marc Bloch, as has been seen, delivered a powerful criticism of an entire generation, and denounced the lack of
"ruthless heroism" among those who directed the fortunes of
France. The charge, made by the Vichy regime and echoed by
some historians, that the politicians were largely responsible for
the defeat of 1940 has been shown to be false: the defeat was
essentially a military defeat, owing to the helpless inability of the
military leaders either to envisage the conduct of modern war or
to execute their own plans smoothly; France was not disarmed or
permitted by her politicians to fall behind in armaments, although none of them challenged the military's view of what was
required or sought to modernize the thinking of the officers.

Some have argued persuasively that even had France
adopted a more aggressive strategy and equipped her forces
with different weapons, and even had she been united internally,
her chances of standing against a more powerful Germany,
without Russia as her ally, were slim. Given the military collapse
of 1940, even a Clemenceau could not have saved the situation in
France, although the struggle might have been continued from
the outposts of the empire; General de Gaulle's activities during

the war effectively accomplished the same end, as parts of the empire rallied to him and French troops were vitally engaged in the liberation of France. As for the canard that the French were so demoralized that the behavior of their troops on the battle-field was less than heroic, it has long since been refuted by the fact that 100,000 men were not killed running away.

The reader should return briefly to the opening pages of this book and reflect upon the critical dossier presented there against the France of the interwar years. Perhaps the arguments and attempted explanations submitted throughout this book will assist him in making his own evaluation of its validity. In our view, there is nothing "strange"—to borrow Marc Bloch's term—about the defeat of 1940, at least in its military, strategic, and diplomatic aspects. Equally there is little that is mysterious about the collapse of the Third Republic: given the military disaster, the near-certainty of Nazi domination over Europe, France's apparently dismal record of division and impotence, and the hangover of hatreds from the turbulent years 1934–1937, the authoritarian alternative had a wide appeal among bewildered and frightened parliamentarians, some of whom, of course, were natural enthusiasts for a regime of authority and order.

If the actual events of 1940 are readily explicable, then the historical problem is of a different character: instead of focusing directly upon the tragedies of 1940 and their immediate antecedents, or "causes," and interpreting the interwar years from the vantage point of 1940, Marc Bloch and countless others who have written about this chapter in French history may be asking us to examine the record of a people and its regime in a particular historical period. But what standards or values should be our guide? The task is treacherous, and possibly without reward. If we accept the participants or contemporary observers as our guide, men like Bloch or Blum, or the men of Vichy or the Resistance, we run the risk of becoming trapped in a web of partisanship. Likewise, if we follow the historians who have concentrated heavily upon the problem of the defeat of 1940, we risk obscuring our understanding of the interwar years as a whole. Certain conclusions, for example, have come all too easily from the pens of historians: by emphasizing the apparent lack of audacity and resolve in foreign affairs, such as at the time of Hitler's reoccupation of the Rhineland in 1936, it may follow that France played a key role in the decomposition of European civilization. On the other hand, France can be seen in quite a different perspective if one simply casts a glance over the Europe of this era, when all of the major continental nations had embraced dictatorship, all destructive of the human personality, and when Great Britain was enduring a period of unrelieved shabbiness; in comparison the record of France becomes immensely more attractive. The dismal lesson of America's involvement in Vietnam may lead us to question the wisdom of those who have denounced France's apparent refusal to defend her vital interests at the risk of war: we might ask was it not more heroic, more humane, indeed more intelligent to seek every way to avoid a new holocaust? One can, then, by choice of argument or of emphasis, offer quite differing interpretations of France in the years 1919–1940.

Granted also that time presents us with different perspectives on every historical epoch, our interpretation is both aided and faulted by our rootedness in our own historical time. Doubtless many historians would prefer to continue asking familiar questions (What happened in 1940? In what ways was France responsible for the accentuation of the international crisis of the 1930s? How could France have prevented the disaster that overtook her?). We have suggested answers to these questions throughout, mindful that definitive answers are elusive and that a multiplicity of factors is inevitably involved in every answer. But our major concern has been to examine the France of the interwar years within a historical framework, by discussing the historical inheritance, such as the Republican synthesis, "stalemated" society, the ideological strands from the past, and the close relationship between political forms and behavior on the one hand and socio-economic reality on the other, in the hope that we have provided the reader with a substantive grasp of the workings and problems of the French Republic.

Certain of our conclusions bear repeating here; obviously

these conclusions are intertwined with the issue of the collapse of France in 1940, and indeed may suggest themselves partly because of that collapse, but they are also independent of it. Most striking is the continuity between the interwar years and the earlier years of the Third Republic: the Republic was a political apparatus that both reflected the compartmentalization of French society and was employed energetically by the bulk of the middle classes and peasantry to preserve that society and the beliefs upon which it rested. The task of the ordinary politician—and there were precious few extraordinary ones—was to protect and defend the achievements of the past and the interests of his special constituency, whether it be his department, electoral district, or a certain sector of society. In other words, every deputy, even the most eminent, took care to protect his clients, to cater to their innate selfishness, and to defend his people against other Frenchmen and partisans of innovation. Thus the state, by general agreement, was limited in its power, and conservatives like Tardieu, who desired a strengthening of the state, and leftists like Blum, who wanted to employ the powers of the state to ameliorate social conditions, were regarded with suspicion and hostility by most of the political class. The politicians were neither prepared nor expected to engage in extraordinary things, nor were they supposed to exhibit statesmanship; when Bloch decried the lack of energy and vision of the parliamentarians, he was denouncing not just individuals, but a whole style of political life. The politicians did what they were expected to do—represent the stalemated society and make small repairs when necessary. Vital repair was postponed and the need often denied, and when economic crisis, social discontent, parliamentary weakness, and the advent of strong and dynamic regimes across the continent combined to produce a super crisis in 1934, the political system was caught unaware and unarmed; hence the extraordinary period of 1934–1937, when all options seemed to be open—fascism, socialism, renewal of democracy, and so on. Yet the political system possessed sufficient vitality to enable it to survive the crisis and by 1938 the fever had passed, although, as we have seen, the legacy of bitterness engendered in 1934–1937 played an important part in the events of 1940 and after.

We have also sought to explain the tenacity of key ideological strands from the nineteenth century by reference to their social implantation as well as by reference to the guardians and manipulators of those strands, such as Charles Maurras or the fascists Doriot and Brasillach. At the same time, we have tried to demonstrate the ways in which the domestic situation affected foreign policy, although it would be foolish to deny the lingering reminder of the First World War and the diplomatic frustrations of the 1920s as factors in the diplomacy of the 1930s. Yet the degree to which internal stresses influenced the conduct of foreign affairs is considerable: many men of the Right, intransigent in the 1920s toward Germany, turned to appeasement of Nazi Germany out of fear of social revolution and Communist Russia, and many men of the Left, ardent pacifists in the 1920s, became willing to wage war to extirpate Nazism and fascism everywhere, especially at home. We have also seen that these tendencies were not inflexible, and many held to their original views.

Finally, we have argued that many of the prevailing social beliefs, shared widely by bourgeois and peasant alike, continued to help shape the French economy, despite the changes required by the needs of the war machine in 1914–1918, the emergence of big production units in the 1920s, the steady reduction of the agricultural population, and the prospects offered by technological innovations. France still preferred, at least in the minds of the majority of her population, to be a land of small and intermediate producers and retailers; very large production and retailing units remained unusual and suspect. For example, supermarkets were attacked by both Right and Left in the 1930s, by the former because they allegedly degraded the dignity of labor and sacrificed quality to quantity, by the latter because they allegedly represented uncontrolled capitalist exploitation. Thus only the beginnings of a modern economy can be detected in the interwar years; in face of Germany's economic mobilization, France's effort can appear only meager.

In many ways, then, France from 1919 to 1940 was imprisoned by her historical inheritance—the political system of the Republic, the social beliefs and fears upon which that system was based, the compartmentalized, stalemated society, and a lingering distaste for economic modernization. Superimposed over this inheritance was the impact of the First World War, although the war had not sufficiently crippled the Republican synthesis and its underpinnings so as to afford a new beginning; the gradual recognition that victory had been an illusion and that the monstrous waste of human life had not provided security were factors shaping the consciousness of every Frenchman in the interwar years. Much else, to be sure, was involved in France's fate—her inability to produce outstanding men or parties, the unreliability of her friends, the unprecedented nature of the challenge from Nazi Germany. But, in large measure, France's situation was the result of her history and the work of her own countrymen. Only a multiple crisis brought about an opportunity to escape from the historical prison in 1934–1937, but the opportunity was wasted.

Yet, despite all of this, France remained a nation that gave allegiance to democracy and the rights of man, and rather than falling easy victim to the so-called dynamic dictatorial alternative, part of the French nation did attempt to reinvigorate the French democratic tradition in 1936–1937 and sought to offer peace to a troubled Europe. Fully admitting that much about the Third Republic in the years from Versailles to Vichy is unappealing today, one cannot deny that, at a dark moment in European history, France remained a land where most men could live in elementary human dignity. That was no small achievement.

Important Persons, Organizations, and Terms

Abbas, Ferhat. Leader of Algerian nationalist organization in the 1930s.

Action Française. Organization of the extreme Right; identified with Charles Maurras.

Alain. Pseudonym of Emile Chartier, philosopher of radicalism.

Auriol, Vincent. Socialist politician; Minister of Finance in 1936–1937.

Barthou, Louis. Foreign Minister; assassinated in 1934; identified with the effort to improve Franco-Soviet relations.

Bloc National. Conservative electoral coalition and government, 1919–1924.

Blum, Léon. Leader of Socialist Party (SFIO), 1921–1940; Premier of Popular Front government, 1936–1937.

Bonnet, Georges. Radical politician; Foreign Minister, 1938–1939; identified with appeasement of Nazi Germany.

Bourguiba, Habib. Leader of Tunisian nationalist movement in the 1930s.

Brasillach, Robert. Novelist and fascist writer.

Briand, Aristide. Several times Premier; Foreign Minister, 1925–1932; identified with conciliatory policy toward Germany.

Bucard, Marcel. Leader of tiny fascist organization, the *Francistes.*

Cagoule. Secret terrorist organization with fascist overtones in the 1930s.

Camelots du Roi. Street gangs of the *Action Française.*

Cartel des Gauches. Socialist and Radical electoral alignment in 1924, and government so called in 1924–1925.

CGT (*Confédération Générale du Travail*). National union organization.

CGTU (*Confédération Générale du Travail Unitaire*). Communist-dominated national union organization.

Chamber of Deputies. Lower house of parliament; elected by universal manhood suffrage.

Chautemps, Camille. Radical politician; several times Premier.

Clemenceau, Georges. Radical politician; authoritarian Premier 1917–1919; leader of French delegation at negotiation of the Versailles Treaty.

Comité des Forges. Organization of the owners of the metallurgical industry.

Congress of Tours, 1920. Famous Socialist Congress at which the party split into two parties, the Socialist and the Communist.

Croix de Feu. Paramilitary league composed largely of war veterans led by Colonel de la Rocque; active in demonstrations on the sixth of February.

Daladier, Edouard. Radical politician; Premier at the time of the riots of the sixth of February 1934 and again at the time of Czechoslovakian crisis; signed for France at Munich conference in 1938; among Radicals he was initially a leader in support of the Popular Front, later a leader against it.

de la Rocque, Colonel François. Leader of the *Croix de Feu,* renamed the *Parti Social Français* in 1936.

Dorgères, Henri. Leader of proto-fascist Green Shirts, which aimed at recruiting peasants.

Doriot, Jacques. Former Communist turned fascist; leader of the largest fascist-type party, the *Parti Populaire Français.*

Doumergue, Gaston. President of the Republic, 1924–1931; called to form a government of "national union" after the riots of the sixth of February 1934.

Drieu la Rochelle, Pierre. Well-known writer with fascist sympathies in the 1930s.

Faure, Paul. General Secretary of the Socialist Party, 1921–1940; leader of its pacifist and anticommunist wing.

Flandin, Pierre-Etienne. Center politician; Premier, 1934–1935; partisan of appeasement in 1938.

Gamelin, General Maurice. Chief of the General Staff, 1935–1940; replaced as Commander by General Weygand in 1940.

Herriot, Edouard. Radical politician; long-time leader of his party; Premier of Cartel government in 1924–1925 and again in 1932.

Hoare-Laval Pact. Abortive agreement between Sir Samuel Hoare, British Foreign Minister, and Premier Laval in 1935, attempting to settle the Italian-Ethiopian conflict on terms very favorable to Italy.

Jaurès, Jean. Pre-1914 Socialist leader whose ideas remained guidelines for postwar Socialist Party; assassinated in 1914.

Jouhaux, Léon. Leader of the CGT, 1921–1940; negotiated the Matignon Agreements in 1936.

Laval, Pierre. Conservative politician; Premier, 1931–1932 and 1935–1936, whose foreign policy, notably toward Italy, aroused much opposition; helped to engineer the end of the Republic at Vichy in 1940.

Lebrun, Albert. President of the Republic, 1932–1940.

Lyautey, Marshal Louis-Hubert. Governor-General of Morocco in the 1920s; attempted to spur modernization of that protectorate.

Maginot Line. Famous defensive fortifications, named after a Minister of Defense; the line ran the length of the Franco-German frontier, but did not stretch across the Franco-Belgian frontier.

Marin, Louis. Conservative politician; leader of the URD (*Union Républicaine Démocratique*).

Matignon Accords. Agreements between management and labor in 1936, negotiated at the Premier's residence, the Hôtel Matignon.

Maulnier, Thierry. Literary critic and fascist activist.

Maurras, Charles. Journalist and political activist; identified with the *Action Française*.

Millerand, Alexandre. Former Socialist turned conservative; identified with the *Bloc National;* President of the Republic, 1920–1924.

National Assembly. Joint meeting of the Chamber of Deputies with the Senate for the purpose of electing a President of the Republic or of making constitutional changes. Meeting at Vichy on July 10, 1940, the National Assembly voted full powers to Marshal Pétain.

Patronat. "Bosses" organization, the CGPF (*Confédération Générale de la Production Française*); negotiated the Matignon Accords of 1936.

Pétain, Marshal Henri-Philippe. Famous general; "victor of Verdun" in the First World War; as Premier, in 1940 won full powers from the National Assembly; presided over the Vichy regime, 1940–1944.

Pivert, Marceau. Left-wing Socialist leader in the 1930s.

Poincaré, Raymond. President of the Republic, 1913–1920; Premier, 1922–1924 and 1926–1929. Most successful politician of the interwar years; during his 1926–1929 ministry, he presided over restoration of confidence in the franc; his earlier ministry was highlighted by the French occupation of the Ruhr, which brought mixed rewards.

Popular Front. Alignment of the Left (Communists, Socialists, and Radicals) in response to the threat of fascism in France; in power, 1936–1937; carried out program of social reform.

Républicains de Gauche. Right-wing political party, to the left of the URD.

Reynaud, Paul. Conservative politician; Finance Minister under Daladier and Premier in 1940; resigned when government voted against his apparent intention to move it to North Africa.

Senate. Upper house of parliament; elected indirectly.

SFIO. (*Section Française de l'Internationale Ouvrière*). Official name of the Socialist Party.

Sixth of February 1934. Date of riots and suspected insurrection against the Republic.

Spinasse, Charles. Socialist politician; Minister of the National Economy in the Blum government; instrumental in persuading parliamentarians to vote full powers to Marshal Pétain in 1940.

Stavisky, Serge. Financial manipulator apparently involved with certain politicians; scandal surrounding his name helped to ignite the riots of the sixth of February 1934.

Tardieu, André. Conservative politician; Premier, 1929–1930 and 1932; desired political, economic, and social reforms.

Thorez, Maurice. Leader of the Communist Party, 1930–1940.

Union Républicaine Démocratique. Right-wing political party, headed by Louis Marin.

Union Sacrée. "Sacred union" of all political parties at the outbreak of the First World War in common cause against the enemy.

Valois, Georges. Leader of a fascist-type organization in the late 1920s.

Weygand, General Maxime. Chief of the General Staff, 1930–1935; called to command the French Army at the moment of its defeat in 1940; insisted that the government ask for an armistice from Hitler.

Zyromski, Jean. Left-wing Socialist politician in the 1930s.

Bibliography

This bibliography attempts to be comprehensive while being selective, and only key articles are mentioned, with emphasis on books in English and French.

GENERAL

Perhaps the best-known of the political histories of the Third Republic is Denis W. Brogan, *The Development of Modern France, 1870–1940* (New York, 1940) and, reissued in paperback edition by Harper & Row, is still eminently readable and useful. Jacques Chastenet's seven-volume *Histoire de la Troisième République* (Paris, 1952–1963) is helpful as an introduction, although the volumes concerned with the interwar years bear a marked conservative bias; the seven-volume *Histoire Politique de la Troisième République* (Paris, 1956–1967) by Georges and Edouard Bonnefous is largely a recounting of events in Parliament and is an excellent reference work. François Goquel's *La Politique des partis sous la Troisième République* (Paris, 1957) views political activities within the framework of two parties, one of "order," the other of "movement," while David Thomson, *Democracy in France* (London, 1952), discusses the evolution of the political strands from the Revolution and nineteenth century in the twentieth. Stanley Hoffmann *et al.*, *In Search of France* (Cambridge, Mass., 1963), contains articles on politics, economics, and society that are essential to an understanding of France in the twentieth century. Three general treatments of the period 1919–1940 in French are useful: Jacques Neré,

La Troisième République, 1914–1940 (Paris, 1967), Claude Fohlen, *La France de l'entre-deux-guerres (1917–1939)* (Paris, 1966), and Léon Cristiani, *La fin d'une régime: tableau de la vie politique française de 1929–1939* (Lyon, 1946). Several articles in James Joll, ed., *The Decline of the Third Republic* (London, 1959), offer insights into French diplomacy, the events of the sixth of February, and the formation of the Popular Front. Two older books, André Siegfried, *France: A Study in Nationality* (New Haven, 1930), and Carlton J. H. Hayes, *France: A Nation of Patriots* (New York, 1930), offer stimulating analytical insights into the workings of French politics and society, and Siegfried's *De la Troisième à la Quatrième République* (Paris, 1957) attempts to place the interwar years in French historical perspective by arguing that these years were quite distinct from the earlier period of the Third Republic. Emmanuel Beau de Loménie's *Les Résponsabilitiés des dynasties bourgeoises* (4 vols.; Paris, 1943–1960) attempts to demonstrate the controlling role played in politics by key financial and industrial interests. The nature of the political system is critically analyzed in Daniel Halévy, *La République des Comités* (Paris, 1934), Robert de Jouvenel, *La République des Camarades* (Paris, 1914, reissued 1934), and André Tardieu, *La Révolution à refaire. Le souverain captif–la profession parlementaire* (Paris, 1937). A handbook of political groupings is Henry Coston, ed., "Partis, journaux et hommes politiques d'hier et d'aujourd'hui," a special number of *Lectures Françaises* for December, 1960. Electoral machinery is discussed by Peter Campbell, *French Electoral Systems and Elections since 1789* (London, 1958), and the results are analyzed by François Goguel in *Geographie des élections françaises de 1870 à 1951* (Paris, 1951). The election results for 1924, 1928, 1932, and 1936 may be found in Georges Lachapelle, *Elections législatives* (4 vols.; Paris, 1924–1936). An excellent historical atlas is René Rémond, directeur, *Atlas historique de la France contemporaine, 1800–1965* (Paris, 1966). The role of the administration is analyzed by Michel Crozier, *The Bureaucratic Phenomenon* (Chicago, 1964), and although devoted to present-day France, Mark Kesselman, *The Ambiguous Consensus: A Study of Local Government in France* (New York, 1967), offers fresh insights into local political decision-making.

ECONOMIC AND SOCIAL

The best study of France's economy during the interwar period is the two-volume work by Alfred Sauvy, *Histoire économique de la France entre les deux guerres* (Paris, 1965–1967), and the dreary details of French finances are made comprehensible in Martin Wolfe, *The French Franc Between the Wars* (New York, 1951). An older, but still useful analysis of the economy is Charles Bettelheim, *Bilan de l'économie française, 1919–1946* (Paris 1947), and the industrial development of the 1920s is discussed by William F. Ogborn and William Jaffe in *The Economic Development of Post-War France* (New York, 1929); attitudes toward business are examined by David S. Landes, "French Business and Businessmen: A Social and Cultural Analysis," in E. M. Earle, ed., *Modern France* (Princeton, 1951), and by Charles P. Kindleberger, *Economic Growth in France and Britain, 1851–1950* (Cambridge, Mass., 1964), and "The Postwar Resurgence of the French Economy" in Stanley Hoffmann *et al.*, *In Search of France* (Cambridge, Mass., 1963). Henry W. Ehrmann, *Organized Business in France* (Princeton, 1957), is an interesting analysis of the role of key businessmen in politics and economics from 1936 to 1955. A good general social history is Georges Dupeux, *La Société française, 1789–1960* (Paris, 1964), and Maurice Duverger has edited a collection of articles on society and politics during the Fourth Republic, *Partis Politiques et Classes Sociales en France* (Paris, 1955), which is useful for an understanding of both in the last years of the Third Republic. French agriculture receives a general treatment by Michel Augé-Laribé, *La Politique agricole de la France de 1850 à 1940* (Paris, 1950), and Pierre Barral, *Les Agrariens français de Méline à Pisani* (Paris, 1968), deals excellently with rural politics at the national level and with peasant organizations. Gordon Wright, *Rural Revolution in France: The Peasantry in the Twentieth Century* (Stanford, 1964), offers a synthetic overview of the years before 1940 and is concerned primarily with developments after 1945. Jean Duplex has edited a splendid atlas, *Atlas de la France rurale* (Paris, 1968). Laurence Wylie has written an excellent study of rural life in the early years of the Fourth Republic, *Village in the Vaucluse* (Cambridge, Mass., 1957), and has edited another, *Chanzeaux: A Village in Anjou* (Cambridge, Mass., 1966). A fine, if fictional, account of village life is *Clochemerle* (Paris, 1964, originally published in 1934) by Gabriel Chevalier. There are four interesting and suggestive regional studies that combine, in differing degree, political, social, and economic history: Pierre Barral, *Le Département de l'Isère sous la Troisième République* (Paris, 1962); Jean-François Viple, *Sociologie politique de l'Allier: la vie politique et les élections sous la Troisième République* (Paris, 1967); Philippe Bernard, *Economie et sociologie de la Seine-et-Marne* (Paris, 1953); and Jean Micheu-Puyou, *Histoire électorale du département des Basses-Pyrénées* (Paris, 1965). A pioneer study in political sociology is André Siegfried, *Tableau politique de la France de l'ouest sous la Troisième République* (Paris, 1913, new edition, 1964). Historical analysis of a key interest group is provided by Charles K. Warner, *The Winegrowers in France and the Government since 1875* (New York, 1960). The best study in English of unions and labor is Val. R. Lorwin, *The French Labor Movement* (Cambridge, Mass., 1954), and the best in French is Georges Lefranc, *Le Mouvement syndical sous la Troisième République* (Paris, 1967); labor in the 1930s is treated by Henry W. Ehrmann in *French Labor, Popular Front to Liberation* (New York, 1947) and by Antoine Prost in his excellent statistical analysis, *La C.G.T. à l'époque du Front Populaire* (Paris, 1964). The first volume of a projected two-volume biography of the union leader Jouhaux has appeared—Bernard Georges and Denise Tintant, *Léon Jouhaux* (Paris, 1962). A very interesting memoir by a union official is André Delmas, *A gauche de la barricade, chronique syndicale de l'avant-guerre* (Paris, 1950).

THE RIGHT AND FASCISM

Considerable attention has been given in recent years to the counterrevolutionary tradition in French politics and in particular to the *Action Française,* but little has appeared as yet on French fascism. The outstanding general treatment is René Rémond, *La Droite en France* (Paris, new edition, 1968), and an excellent article on the French Right by Eugen Weber may be found in Eugen Weber and Hans Rogger, eds., *The European Right: A Historical Profile* (Berkeley and Los Angeles, 1965). Charles Maurras and the *Action Française* are the objects of two excellent studies, Eugen Weber, *Action Française* (Stanford, 1962), and Ernst Nolte, *Three Faces of Fascism* (New York, 1966); Edward R. Tannenbaum, *The Action Française* (New York, 1962), and Samuel Osgood, *French Royalism under the Third and Fourth Republics* (The Hague, 1960), also merit attention. The best treatment of the Right in the 1930s, especially with regard to foreign policy, is Charles A. Micaud, *The French Right and Nazi Germany* (Durham, N. C., 1943). Fascism has been studied by Jean Plumyène and Raymond Lasierra in *Les Fascismes français, 1923–1963* (Paris, 1963), and by Paul Sérant, *Le Romantisme fasciste* (Paris, 1959). Perhaps the best synthetic analyses of French fascism are the articles by Robert J. Soucy, "The Nature of Fascism in France" in *The Journal of Contemporary History,* No. 1, 1966, reprinted in Nathanael Greene, ed., *Fascism: An Anthology* (New York, 1968), and Raoul Giradet, "Note sur l'esprit d'un fascisme français, 1934–1939," in *Revue Française de Science Politique,* V (July–September 1955). Colonel de la Rocque and his *Croix de Feu* have not yet found their historian, although Philippe Rudaux, *Les Croix de feu et le P.S.F.* (Paris, 1967), represents a beginning. There is no substantial work on Jacques Doriot; Doriot's *La France avec nous* (Paris, 1937) and *Refaire la France* (Paris, 1938) contain the essence of his politics. An early fascist, Georges Valois, is the subject of a stimulating article by Yves Guchet, "Georges Valois ou l'illusion fasciste" in *Revue Française de Science Politique*

XV (December 1965). Theose interested in Robert Brasillach should read his *Notre avant-guerre* (Paris, 1941).

THE LEFT

The starting point for an understanding of radicalism during the interwar years is Alain (pseudinym of Emile Chartier), *Eléments d'une doctrine radicale* (Paris, 1925), and the only systematic study of the party is Peter J. Larmour, *The French Radical Party in the 1930's* (Stanford, 1964). Edouard Herriot has found a skillful and sympathetic biographer in Michel Soulié, *La Vie politique d'Edouard Herriot* (Paris, 1962), and Herriot's memoirs, *Jadis,* Vol. II, *D'une guerre à l'autre, 1914–1936* (Paris, 1952), are worth examination. Herriot's little brochure, *Pourquoi je suis radical-socialiste* (Paris, 1928), is instructive. Edouard Daladier has written no memoirs, and his *In Defense of France* (New York, 1939) is a collection of speeches; Camille Chautemps wrote a thin memoir dealing with the events of 1939–1940 entitled *Cahiers secrets de l'armistice* (Paris, 1963). For socialism, the best general work is Georges Lefranc, *Le Mouvement socialiste sous la Troisième République* (Paris, 1963); the volume by Daniel Ligou, *Histoire du socialisme en France, 1871–1961* (Paris, 1962), should be avoided whenever possible. The career and legacy of Jean Jaurès are treated by Harvey Goldberg in *The Life of Jean Jaurès* (Madison, Wisc., 1962), and the vicissitudes of socialism during the First World War are brilliantly examined by Robert Wohl in *French Communism in the Making, 1914–1924* (Stanford, 1966) and by Annie Kriegel in *Aux Origines du communisme français, 1914–1920* (2 vols.; Paris, 1964). The Socialist Party in the 1930s has been analyzed by John T. Marcus, *French Socialism in the Crisis Years, 1933–1936* (New York, 1958), and by Nathanael Greene, *Crisis and Decline: The French Socialist Party in the Popular Front Era* (Ithaca, N.Y., 1969). The best biography of Léon Blum is Joel Colton, *Léon Blum: Humanist in Politics* (New York, 1966), although the studies by Louise E. Dalby, *Léon Blum: Evolution of a Socialist* (New York, 1963), and James Joll, *Intellectuals in Politics* (London, 1960), deserve mention. Blum's most important writings, including newspaper articles, have been collected by several editors in *L'Oeuvre de Léon Blum* (7 vols.; Paris, 1955–1965). Blum's introspective analysis of the defeat of France and of the failings of French socialism, *A l'échelle humaine* (Paris, 1945), has been translated by W. Pickles as *For All Mankind* (New York, 1946). Gilbert Ziebura's political biography of Blum, originally published in German, has been translated as *Léon Blum et le parti socialiste, 1872–1934* (Paris, 1967), and the papers presented by scholars at a recent meeting devoted to the Blum government in 1936–1937 have been published under the title *Léon Blum, chef de gouvernement, 1936–1937* (Paris, 1967). There is no biography of Paul Faure: those interested in his career should consult his *Au Seuil d'une révolution* (Limoges, 1934) and his little volume of memoirs, *De Munich à la Ve République* (Paris, 1948). On the development of communism and the Communist Party, in addition to the works of Wohl and Kriegel already cited, the best general history is by Jacques Fauvet, *Histoire du Parti Communiste français*, Vol. I (Paris, 1965), and a useful study of the party in the Popular Front period is Daniel Brower, *The New Jacobins: The French Communist Party and the Popular Front* (Ithaca, N.Y., 1968). The Communist interpretation of the Popular Front is ably expressed by the party leader Maurice Thorez, *France Today and the People's Front* (New York, n.d.), and by Jacques Chambaz, *Le Front Populaire pour le pain, la liberté, et la paix* (Paris, 1961). The attraction of communism for intellectuals is explained by David Caute, *Communism and the French Intellectuals, 1914–1960* (New York, 1964), and in the excellent book by Georges Lichtheim, *Marxism in Modern France* (New York, 1966); the opening chapters of Charles A. Micaud, *Communism and the French Left* (New York, 1963), are of interest.

THE FIRST WORLD WAR AND THE ARMY

The literature devoted to the First World War is immense; the reader should consult the general synthetic history by Cyril Falls, *The Great War, 1914–1918* (New York, 1959). Relations between the parliament and the military are scrutinized by Jere C. King, *Generals and Politicians* (Berkeley and Los Angeles, 1951), and the development of the state in wartime is traced by Pierre Renouvin, *The Forms of War Government in France* (New Haven, 1927); Renouvin has also written about the armistice of 1918, *L'Armistice de Rethondes* (Paris, 1968), and the mutinies in the French Army in 1917 are detailed by Guy Pedroncini, *Les Mutineries de 1917* (Paris, 1968). The role of the Army in peacemaking in 1919 is analyzed by Jere C. King, *Foch versus Clemenceau* (Cambridge, Mass., 1960). An adequate general history of the Army is Paul-Marie de la Gorce, *The French Army: A Military-Political History* (New York, 1963), and the development of the Army's strategic and ideological outlook is analyzed by Philip C. F. Bankwitz, *Maxime Weygand and Civil-Military Relations in Modern France* (Cambridge, Mass., 1967). The memoirs of General Maxime Weygand, *Mémoires* (3 vols.; Paris, 1950–1957), and of General Maurice Gamelin, *Servir* (3 vols.; Paris, 1946–1947), are of interest to the general reader as well as the specialist.

DIPLOMACY

An older but still useful general treatment is Arnold Wolfers, *Britain and France Between Two Wars* (New York, 1940), and Frederick Schumann, *War and Diplomacy in the French Republic* (New York, 1931), remains valuable for the diplomacy of the 1920s. Two outstanding works by Arno J. Mayer, *Political Origins of the New Diplomacy, 1917–1918* (New Haven, 1959), and *Politics and Diplomacy of Peacemaking* (New York, 1967), offer valuable insights into the workings of French diplomacy in the last year of the First World War and at the peace conference in 1919. Jean-Baptiste Duroselle, France's leading diplomatic historian with the retirement of Pierre Renouvin, offers a course at the Sorbonne on Franco-German relations from 1914–1939, and his lectures have been published, in three small volumes, as

Les Relations franco-allemandes de 1914 à 1939 (Paris, 1967); Duroselle has also written an excellent article on the Rhineland crisis of 1936, translated by Nancy L. Roelker, "France and the Crisis of March 1936," in Evelyn Acomb and Marvin Brown, eds., *French Society and Culture Since the Old Regime* (New York, 1966). The study by William S. Evans, *Alliance Against Hitler: The Origins of the Franco-Soviet Pact* (Durham, N. C., 1963), is useful. The career of Aristide Briand has been examined in great detail by Georges Suarez, *Briand* (6 vols.; Paris, 1938–1952); the diplomacy of Pierre Laval receives sketchy treatment by Geoffrey Warner, *Pierre Laval and the Eclipse of France 1931–1945* (New York, 1968); and the other Minister of Foreign Affairs of note, Georges Bonnet, has written an able but not convincing account of his diplomacy, *Fin d'une Europe, De Munich à la Guerre* (Geneva, 1948, reissued in Paris, 1967). Alexis Léger, Secretary General of the Foreign Office, is the subject of the fine article by Elizabeth R. Cameron, "Alexis Saint-Léger," in Gordon Craig and Felix Gilbert, eds., *The Diplomats* (Princeton, 1953). Three books deal extensively with France and the crisis over Czechoslovakia: Alexander Werth, *France and Munich* (New York, 1939); Keith Eubank, *Munich* (Norman, Okla., 1963); and J. W. Wheeler-Bennett, *Munich: Prologue to Tragedy* (London, new edition, 1963). A. J. P. Taylor, *The Origins of the Second World War* (London, 1961), must be read. Two of France's ablest ambassadors have written their memoirs: Robert Coulondre, *De Staline à Hitler: Souvenirs de deux ambassades, 1936–1939* (Paris, 1950), and André François-Poncet, *Souvenirs d'une ambassade à Berlin, septembre 1931–octobre 1938* (Paris, 1946). The publication of French diplomatic documents has begun only recently, with the exception of *Le Livre jaune français. Documents diplomatiques, 1938–1939* (Paris, 1939), an official publication of the Foreign Ministry. Documents are being published under the title *Documents diplomatiques français, 1932–1939* in two series: the first for 1932–1935, the second for 1936–1939. Volumes have appeared for 1932 and 1936 (Paris, 1964–1966).

THE 1930s

In addition to the works cited under other headings, there are several valuable studies of the events of the 1930s. Alexander Werth, Paris correspondent of the *Manchester Guardian,* wrote "a first-class political chronicle," as D. W. Brogan put it, of the 1930s. Werth's several books were skillfully abridged into *The Twilight of France* (New York, 1942), which was reissued, happily, in 1966. After the Second World War, the National Assembly authorized an inquiry into the events of the years 1933–1945, and the commission charged with the task interviewed many of the leading personalities of the interwar years, such as Blum, Daladier, and Sarraut. Their testimony and the conclusions of the commission were published in nine volumes as *Rapport fait au nom de la commission d'enquête sur les événements survenus en France de 1933 à 1945* (Paris, 1951). The events of the sixth of February 1934 were also the object of an official inquiry published by the Chamber of Deputies, *Rapport général fait au nom de la commission d'enquête chargée de rechercher les causes et les origines des événements du 6 février 1934* (Paris, 1934). Max Beloff's article "The Sixth of February" in James Joll, ed., *The Decline of the Third Republic* (New York, 1959) is a balanced and sensible analysis; Maurice Chavardès, *Le six février 1934* (Paris, 1966), is designed for a popular audience. The best history of the Popular Front is Georges Lefranc, *Histoire du Front Populaire* (Paris, 1965), and the study by a left-wing Socialist, Daniel Guérin, *Front Populaire, Révolution Manquée* (Paris, 1963), captures the enthusiasm of the Popular Front. Another excellent study is Georges Dupeux, *Le Front Populaire et les élections de 1936* (Paris, 1959); a popular history is Jean Grandmougin, *Histoire vivante de Front Populaire, 1934–1939* (Paris, 1966). The sit-in strikes have been analyzed by Jacques Danos and Marcel Gibelin, *Juin 1936* (Paris, 1952), and by Antoine Prost, "Les grèves de juin 1936, essai d'interprétation," in *Léon Blum, chef de gouvernement, 1936–1937,* already cited. An interesting documentary collection on the strikes is Georges Lefranc, *Juin 36* (Paris, 1966).

BIOGRAPHIES AND MEMOIRS NOT ALREADY CITED

Geoffrey Bruun, *Clemenceau* (Cambridge, Mass., 1945); Georges Clemenceau, *Grandeurs et misères d'une victoire* (Paris, 1930); Joseph Paul-Boncour, *Entre deux guerres: souvenirs sur la Troisième République* (3 vols.; Paris, 1945–1946); Pierre Miquel, *Poincaré* (Paris, 1961); Rudolph Binion, *Defeated Leaders: The Political Fate of Caillaux, de Jouvenel, and Tardieu* (New York, 1960); Pierre-Etienne Flandin, *Politique française, 1919–1940* (Paris, 1947); Pierre Cot, *The Triumph of Treason* (New York, 1944); and Paul Reynaud, *Mémoires* (Paris, 1963).

THE PRESS

A general treatment is Raymond Manévy, *La Presse de la Troisième République* (Paris, 1955). The "Kiosque" series presents excerpts from the press on selected themes or events, and four are of interest: René Rémond, *Les Catholiques, le communisme, et les crises, 1929–1939* (Paris, 1960); Louis Bodin and Jean Touchard, *Front Populaire 1936* (Paris, 1961); Pierre Milza, *L'Italie fasciste devant l'opinion française 1920–1940* (Paris, 1967); and Geneviève Vallette and Jacques Bouillon, *Munich 1938* (Paris, 1964). Jacques Kayser has edited a number of articles on the press under the title *La Presse de province sous la Troisième République* (Paris, 1958), and Françoise Mayeur has studied a minor Paris journal in *"L'Aube," Etude d'un journal d'opinion, 1932–1940* (Paris, 1966). The *Annuaire de la Presse* lists Parisian and provincial newspapers and their circulation, and the Periodical Department of the Bibliothèque Nationale has begun to issue bound catalogues of provincial newspapers by department, under the general title *Bibliographie de la presse française politique et d'information générale, 1865–1944*. Students beginning research on the interwar period should consult the *Journal Officiel de la République Française* for the stenographic record of debates in the Chamber of Deputies and the Senate, and the newspapers *Le Temps* (conservative), *Le Populaire*

(Socialist SFIO), *l'Humanité* (Communist), *La Dépêche de Toulouse* (Radical), *l'Action Française,* and *Gringoire* (extreme Right) are available on microfilm at many universities in the United States. An extensive annotated bibliography of the press may be found in Carlton J. H. Hayes, *France: A Nation of Patriots,* cited previously.

THE DEFEAT OF 1940

The literature is vast, and the titles given here are meant to be suggestive, and not definitive. An excellent short article by Richard D. Challener, "The Military Defeat of 1940 in Retrospect," is found in Craig and Gilbert, eds., *Modern France,* cited previously. The military disaster is ably recounted by Colonel A. Goutard, *The Battle of France, 1940* (New York, 1959), and by General André Beaufre, *1940—The Fall of France* (New York, 1968). Jacques Benoist-Méchin, identified with the Vichy regime, has written a chronicle entitled *Sixty Days That Shook the West* (New York, 1963). New books by Guy Chapman, *Why France Fell* (New York, 1969), Alistair Horne, *To Lose a Battle* (New York, 1969), and William L. Shirer, *The Collapse of the Third Republic* (New York, 1969), deal with the military problems at length; Marc Bloch, *The Strange Defeat,* is now available in a paperback edition (New York, 1968). Pertinax, *The Gravediggers of France* (New York, 1944), is a harsh book devoted to Gamelin, Daladier, Reynaud, Pétain, and Laval. Memoirs by Gamelin, Weygand, and Chautemps have already been cited; Paul Reynaud, *In the Thick of the Fight* (New York, 1955), and General Charles de Gaulle, *The Call to Honour* (New York, 1955), must be consulted. The collapse of the Third Republic at Vichy on July 10 is ably described in Robert Aron, *The Vichy Regime* (New York, 1958), Henri Michel, *Vichy, Année 1940* (Paris, 1966), and Emmanuel Berl, *La Fin de la Troisième République* (Paris, 1968).

FRENCH CULTURE BETWEEN THE WARS

An excellent analysis of the 1930s may be found in H. Stuart Hughes, *The Obstructed Path: French Social Thought in the Years of Desperation, 1930–1960* (New York, 1968). General literary surveys include: Henri Clouard, *Histoire de la littérature française du symbolisme à nos jours* (2 vols.; Paris, 1947–1949); André Rousseaux, *Littérature du XXe siècle* (Paris, 1949); Pierre Brodin, *Les écrivains français de l'entre-deux-guerres* (Montreal, 1943), and Henri Peyre, *The Contemporary French Novel* (New York, 1955). An interesting study of a great novelist is David L. Schalk, *Roger Martin du Gard, the Novelist and History* (Ithaca, N.Y., 1967). Without giving a long and unrewarding list of works from the period, we must cite Georges Bernanos, *A Diary of My Times* (New York, 1938); Antoine de Saint-Exupéry, *Night Flight* (New York, 1945); André Malraux, *Man's Hope* (New York, 1938); Paul Nizan, *La Conspiration* (Paris, 1938); and André Gide, *Retour de l'URSS* (Paris, 1936).

Religious history is ably treated by Adrien Dansette, *Histoire religieuse de la France contemporaine* (2 vols.; Paris, 1951), and *Destin du catholicisme français, 1926–1956* (Paris, 1957). Colonial history in the interwar years has been seriously neglected: Stephen H. Roberts, *A History of French Colonial Policy* (London, 1926), is barely useful; Albert Sarraut, onetime Governor-General of Indo-China, wrote *Grandeur et servitude coloniales* (Paris, 1926); M. Allain, *Notre belle France d'outremer* (Paris, 1934), is what its title suggests; Jean-Brunhes Delamarre, *La France dans le monde, ses colonies, son empire* (Tours, 1940), is a useful survey; and Henri Deschamps, *Les Méthodes et les doctrines coloniales de la France* (Paris, 1953), is very helpful.

Index

155